"From the very beginning, God's design for discipleship was with parents in mind. Sam highlights an important shift that needs to happen in next-gen ministries today and this book has the practical tools and first-hand experience to show you how! A must-read for any team looking to elevate parents back into their God-designed roles."

Emmanuel Caraballo, Next-Gen Pastor

"Growing our lens of youth ministry from a ministry to teens to a ministry to the whole family is a must. ParentEquip lays out the principles and practical steps needed for Next-Gen leaders to grow better in our service to families. Parents will feel more empowered and better equipped to lead their families through the beautiful tips given through these teachings."

Will Perry, Lead Student Pastor

"As both a parent and Next-Gen Pastor of 15 years, I believe ParentEquip is a must for the church if we want to see our children thrive in this current culture as life-long followers of Jesus."

Gary Casaletto, Next-Gen Pastor

"ParentEquip is a practical and inspiring resource. Definitely a great book to motivate and equip your entire Next-Gen team to partner with parents!

Daryl and Trisha Allen, Next-Gen Pastors

"I deeply admire Sam's holistic approach to Next-Gen ministry. Kids/youth pastors who don't (yet) have a strategy to empower parents are doing ministry with one arm tied behind their back. This resource is designed to help you unleash your ministry's full potential impact on this generation and bear fruit that truly remains."

Cody Duff, Next-Gen Pastor

"Empowering parents is a must in Next-Gen ministry! The principles that Sam outlines are both biblical and practical, providing a helpful perspective on the Biblical model of empowering families."

Will Hutcherson, Co-Author of *SEEN* and *Beyond the Spiral*

ParentEquip

A Next-Gen Leader Guide to

*Reinstating Parents as the
Primary Spiritual Leaders*

Sam McDowell

ParentEquip

Copyright © 2023 by Sam McDowell

All rights reserved. No part of this book may be reproduced or transmitted in any form or by any means, electronic or mechanical, including photocopying, recording, or by any information storage and retrieval system without express written permission from the author, except in the case of brief quotations embodied in critical reviews and certain other noncommercial uses permitted by copyright law.

Note: Names in the stories told throughout this book have been changed out of respect and protection for those involved. I am grateful for and honor every student and parent who has given me the opportunity to help lead them through next generation ministry.

ISBN 979-8-218-24752-2 (softcover)

Printed in the United States of America.

Table of Contents

Part One: Introduction

    Chapter 1: The Beginning. .1

    Chapter 2: The Biblical Case for ParentEquip 7

    Chapter 3: The Example of the Early Church 17

    Chapter 4: God's Design for Families 29

Part Two: The Strategy

    Chapter 5: (Foundation #1) 45

    Chapter 6: (Foundation #2) 67

    Chapter 7: (Foundation #3). 81

Part Three: The Application

    Chapter 8: The Fruit of ParentEquip
    in Your Ministry. 101

    Chapter 9: Leading Your Ministry Forward. 105

Part One: Introduction

Chapter 1: The Beginning

I will never forget the moment I realized I was more than a youth pastor. I was lying prone behind my bolt action long gun, looking downrange at my target five-hundred and thirty yards out. Slowly steadying my breath, with my crosshairs on target, I began to move my finger to the trigger, when I heard a voice to my right say, "Sam, can I ask you a question?" Garrett, the father of one of the students I pastored, and I had been shooting together for months on a private rifle range after church on Sundays. He had just packed up his gear and was leaning against his SUV, looking uneasy but eager. "What am I doing wrong with Andrew?"

Just seconds before, I was intently focused on my target downrange, but now Garrett had my full attention. I've come to realize that this is a common question for parents, but at the time, I have to admit that it shocked me a bit. Garrett was not only a father and husband but a soldier who spent the last two decades serving as a military and contract sniper. To me, he was the picture of confidence. When I first met Garrett, I knew I wanted to get to know him because of his background, but at the same time, I was quite intimidated by him. Standing well over 6 feet tall, with a full, thick beard, upright posture, and the tough confidence you'd probably expect from a military veteran, the way he carried himself was not exactly what I'd call "approachable." And each week, I saw him and his family come to church and leave as soon as service was dismissed. In my mind, they didn't seem like they needed any help.

Garrett's son Andrew was a junior at the local high school, and he had the "it" factor. Outgoing, magnetic personality, athlete, popular kid, respectful but edgy, etc. I felt like I had to go out of my way to connect with him and his family, but after weeks of hustling this kid to come to our youth ministry, he finally showed up—with all of his friends. Over the next couple months, I saw Andrew flourish. He plugged into a small group in our ministry and began making some new Christian friends while still remaining connected to his school friends. As he got more involved with our youth ministry, I knew it was time to try to connect with his father. That's how I ended up inviting Garrett to come to the gun range with me on Sundays after church. While I've never served in the military, I have always been interested in the special operations community, and I have pursued long-range precision shooting as a hobby. In light of Garrett's background, I thought we could make a great connection on the gun range.

At first, our conversations were pretty stilted. I asked a lot of questions to try to get to know Garrett and show interest in his story, but he typically replied with short answers. It was like trying to draw water out of a dry well. Over time, however, things began to shift. Our conversations got richer, broaching deeper topics and sharing personal details. I soon learned that while Garett had a tough exterior, he had a ton of sensitivity and depth. I learned that he struggled with knowing who he was after walking away from two decades of service overseas, that his identity in some ways remained at his final assignment as a contractor. He shared how guilty he felt missing so many years with his kids while simultaneously feeling completely paralyzed now that he was home for good, not knowing how to move forward. He even shared that he thought his marriage might be too far gone after everything they'd been through. I'm so grateful that our friendship grew to this depth of trust and vulnerability, because one day, he felt comfortable enough to ask, "What am I doing wrong with Andrew?" That simple, vulnerable question ignited a passion in me that led me to create the ParentEquip strategy and write this book.

Garrett's question reflects the honest fear and insecurity burdening the heart of almost every parent trying to raise a kid in our world today. All parents tend to have similar core internal dialogues. *How do I handle this? Am I doing enough? How do I know that I'm doing the right thing?* These sentiments play on repeat in parents' minds–but what makes our job as next generation leaders difficult is that they often don't ask for help.

Over the last few years, I've talked with dozens of parents of adult children who just shake their heads in disbelief at the things parents are having to navigate through in today's society. Wading through the murky waters of an ever-changing, overwhelming world that seems intent on influencing our kids is brutal. Parents are simply trying to keep their heads above water and don't really know where to turn, even if they do have the capacity to ask for help. Some struggle to admit they need help, but that doesn't mean they don't have a deep desire to lead their children well. If you're reading this book, you're most likely a leader who works in Next Generation ministry. You know that this societal reality is true. Raising kids is more difficult today than ever before, and parents need our **help** to succeed at leading their children to become fully devoted followers of Jesus.

But it's vital for us to recognize that *help* is the key word! The current landscape of next generation ministry in the western church positions youth and kids ministers to function as the greatest spiritual influence in the lives of young people, but I believe God never intended for it to be this way. I've written this book to help empower your ministry with a deeply Biblical strategy that reinstates parents in their rightful, God-given role of spiritual leadership. God wants parents to be bold and passionate about leading their kids into a rich and personal life of discipleship with Jesus, and our job is to help equip parents for this ministry. I urge you to read this entire book to see how the ParentEquip strategy can position your ministry to partner with parents in a way that develops your students into life-long followers of Jesus.

Back to Garrett and Andrew. Still lying next to my bolt gun on the range, I looked up at Garrett and gently told him that there was a significant disconnect (broken intimacy) between him and his son because Andrew was afraid of him. I shared that Andrew didn't feel safe to come to him about anything. I stood up, looked Garrett in the eyes, and said, "If you can create a safe place for your son, the gap between you will begin to close. When Andrew feels safe, he will open up to you in ways you wouldn't believe." Essentially, I was encouraging Garrett to do with Andrew what I had done with Garrett. Building safety and trust creates space for leadership and impact.

The very next morning, I had breakfast with Andrew. As we ate, he told me that in church that Sunday, he felt the Holy Spirit encouraging him to tell his dad about his drug addiction, and while he was nervous and hesitant, he knew that he needed to be obedient. Just hours after Garrett and I had been together at the range, he had confessed to his dad. And Andrew said his father had stood up and wrapped him in a huge embrace. After a moment, Garrett leaned back from Andrew, and, looking him in the eyes, said, "Son, I want you to know that I love you. I am so thankful you shared this with me, and I want you to know that we will defeat this addiction together." Andrew told me over our Chick-Fil-A breakfast that morning that this was the first time he could remember his dad hugging him or telling him he loved him.

Imagine the difference this moment made in Garrett and Andrew's relationship, the door it opened for Garrett to have a new speaking role in his son's life. Think of how God could use Garrett to point Andrew to Him. This, my friend, is the perfect picture of ParentEquip: equipping, empowering parents to step into their biblical role as the spiritual leader of their child's life. I believe this is God's design for families and the spiritual development of the next generation. While the effort we put into molding young people through youth and kids ministries is incredibly important, I believe we can make an even greater impact if we shift some of our focus towards parents.

This doesn't mean we take a step back as leaders in our students' lives! We still meet with them, go to performances and sporting events, gather them together for game nights and show up when they need us to! We just need to adopt a new philosophy that positions parents to be the heroes in their kid's story. The people students look to first for support and biblical wisdom. I am not in any way proposing that we as church leaders should back away to a dormant position. If anything, I am asking us to engage even more, just with a slightly different focus. I believe our true calling as Next Gen leaders is to bridge the gap between parents and their kids and to restore God's intended spiritual order for leadership and discipleship.

I know I am biased, but I feel there are few calls greater than this. We have the ability to leverage our relationships, influence, and gifts from the Lord to reconcile the family unit back to what God originally designed it to be. Instead of being primary spiritual leaders for the next generation, we can be restoration experts for families.

Throughout the rest of this book, you will see that I am not suggesting a huge overhaul in the way we approach student or kids ministry. In fact, many of the strategies I discuss will sound familiar or may already be a part of your ministry. The key is *combining* these strategies with the mission to equip parents to become the spiritual leaders in the lives of their children. God will use this combination of great Next Gen ministry and ParentEquip to impact the families in your ministry in profound, life-changing ways. I pray that as you continue to read, God will give you passion and vision to restore families like never before.

Chapter 2:
The Biblical Case for ParentEquip

Before we get any further into this book, I want to look at truths from Scripture that form the biblical foundation of ParentEquip. I believe this strategy of working to restore spiritual leadership in families is biblically sound and close to the heart of God.

It's a little uncomfortable to say, and maybe a little uncomfortable to hear, but God never created youth or kids' ministries. God's design and continued desire is for parents to walk confidently in their role as the *primary* spiritual leaders in the lives of their children. We can see from the beginning with the early church that God intended for the spiritual growth of a young person to be cultivated and developed primarily by their parents, not by the pastor down the road. Now, I'm not at all downplaying the importance of the local church. I have served in vocational ministry in the local church my entire adult life and will continue to do so as long as God wants me to. But I do believe we need a shift in the local church to begin to think differently about the way we organize our ministries.

Let me explain. More often than not, the lead pastor of a church leads the adult generations while the kids' and youth pastors lead the younger generations. Adult congregants are often simply consumers, leaving church "fed" on Sundays but not recognizing their *feeding* role. The older generation has an assignment from God–not just to consume spiritual content but to steward what they learn by sowing it into their children. The western church has created a model that emphasizes the importance of older generations depending on the pastor, without reinforcing the importance of a child's dependence upon the parent (which has also sadly led to the loss of valuing the influence of grandparents and great grandparents). This is a tragedy and deviation from God's original intent for families! As church leaders, we should endeavor to help parents own the primary spiritual role by not only educating them spiritually but equipping them to connect their spiritual knowledge to their leadership role in the family. We have to connect parents not only to the Word of God, but also to their mandate as parents.

Let's look at a few specific Scriptures that reveal God's desire for parents to fulfill their role as the primary spiritual leaders in the lives of their children.
In Deuteronomy 6:7-9, immediately following the 10 Commandments, God gives parents specific directions to take the commands that He's given us and pass them to our children: "You shall teach them diligently to your children, and shall talk of them when you sit down *in your house*, and when you walk by the way, and when you lie down, and when you rise. You shall bind them as a sign on your hand, and they shall be as frontlets between your eyes. You shall write them *on your doorposts* of your house and on

your gates" (NKJV, emphasis added). This Scripture is so rich and shows us that God intended for the home to be where children were taught the ways of God, day in and day out. Let's take a moment to break these verses down to see the significance of a parent's role in a child's life when it comes to spiritual discipleship.

"*Teach them diligently...*" (verse 7).

The above passage immediately follows the verse in Deuteronomy 6 that states, "and these words that I command to you today shall be on your hearts." The word "diligently" in verse 7 is a Hebrew word that means "to sharpen, whet or pierce." Think about it for a moment: Intentionally repeating something over and over again instills the idea in the mind and makes it pierce the heart as firm truth. Proverbs 4:23 (ESV) instructs us to "Keep [our] heart with all vigilance, for from it flow the springs of life." Luke 6:45 shows us that the person with good treasure in their heart is the one that produces good. What if the diligence God commands of parents in Deuteronomy 6:7 is the very thing that, over time, causes His truth to pierce the heart of a child with the truth of God? This "heart piercing" diligence requires repetition. It requires consistent proximity. Who are the people God placed in the lives of children with the proximity and ability to repeat truth to their kids every single day? **Parents**. God's plan was for families to build and preserve a legacy of faith with a deep, significant faith in God and His Word, passed down from generation to generation.

The next couple of verses lay out a few practical ways for parents to walk this out:

> "...and shall talk of them when you sit down in your house, and when you walk by the way, and when you lie down, and when you rise up" (verse 7).

This verse is essentially saying, "Talk about the things of God *all the time!*" But sadly, most families are hardly spending any quality time together these days. Parents rarely sit down at the dinner table enough. If they do, distractions like cell phones, social media, and television in the background can often take away the opportunity for intentional conversation. A lack of margin in schedules makes mornings and evenings feel like the Indy 500 just to get to places on time. Bedtimes are rushed, stressful, and lacking intentionality. Mornings are chaotic. Some parents are exhausted from the pace of life and cannot get out of bed while others are out of the house at hyper-speed to get to work early. But "diligently" piercing the heart of a child with God's truth takes focused attention, margin, and effort. Given the pace and stress of life, it's no wonder parents have passed the spiritual development of their children to the local church. Time is a resource most parents do not have in abundance, given the pace and pressures of life in today's society. As next generation leaders, we have to know the *families* in our ministry, not just the kids. We have to get into their world and help instruct parents, educate them, and encourage them to recognize that they have a greater calling than the everyday hustle of life. Why? Because their child's heart, faith, and eternity hang in the balance. The Christian faith remaining in their family for generations is largely dependent on their faithfulness to their parental role. Don't forget: The Lord did not follow up the commandments by exhorting priests to do their job. He exhorted parents to do theirs.

> *"You shall bind them as a sign on your hand, and they shall be as frontlets between your eyes. You shall write them on your doorposts of your house and on your gates"* (verses 8-9).

Remember that at the time of this command, God had only *just* given the 10 Commandments to Moses. There were no other copies of the law. And even once copies began to be made, access to the Holy Scriptures was certainly not readily available the way it is today. The people of Israel really only heard Scripture read at the Feast of Tabernacles. Imagine going to hear the Word of God and your only way to remember it was writing it on parchment to wear around your wrists or committing it to memory and engraving it in your home for your family to see. This took enormous intentionality, but it was the only way to teach children the law of the Lord. As I mentioned at the beginning of this chapter, we should help parents own the primary role by not only educating them spiritually but equipping them to <u>connect their spiritual knowledge to their responsibility to disciple their children</u>." The people of Israel had to take this charge seriously, and so should we.

This was God's plan then, and I firmly believe it remains His plan today. He will always choose a father or mother as the first ideal to raise up a child in truth. Of course, you and I know that He graciously uses others like us to help mentor young people spiritually as they grow, but we have too high of an opinion of ourselves as ministry leaders if we think God would prefer to use us to influence students more than their parents. Instead, we should focus on empowering parents to fill this incredibly important role in their children's lives!

Psalm 78:1-7 reflects on these commands from God in Deuteronomy 6 and paints a beautiful picture of one generation passing faith down to another.

> *"Give ear, O my people, to my law; incline your ears to the words of my mouth. I will open my mouth in a parable; I will utter dark sayings of old, which we have heard and known, and our fathers have told us. We will not hide them from their children, telling to the generation to come the praises of the Lord, and His strength and His wonderful works that He has done. For He established a testimony in Jacob, and appointed a law in Israel, which He commanded our fathers, That they should make them known to their children; That the generation to come might know them, the children who would be born, that they may arise and declare them to their children, That they may set their hope in God, and not forget the works of God, but keep His commandments"* (KJV).

Asaph was the great musician of David and Solomon's era. He was a prophetic voice through the composition of lyrics and music. Asaph begins the psalm acknowledging that the content of his lyrics would not be new ideas to the reader. *"I will utter dark sayings of old, which we have heard and known, and our fathers have told us."* While

Asaph's prophetic voice held weight and was being used by God to communicate law and truth, he was simply recalling and reiterating truth his readers already knew. And why did they already know? Because in those times, fathers faithfully passed on the holy law to their children. Simply put, Asaph's words in Psalm 78 were designed to be a supplement, not a substitute. Charles Spurgeon said it this way; "The more of parental teaching the better; ministers and Sabbath-school teachers were never meant to be substitutes for mother's tears and father's prayers."

Asaph reinforces this idea in verse 4: "We will not hide them from their children, telling to the generation to come the praises of the Lord, and His strength and His wonderful works that He has done." Parents had the responsibility to not hide from their children what had once been passed down to them by their own parents. This touches on a multi-generational deposit of faith that is emphasized even more in verses 5-7: *"For He established a testimony in Jacob, and appointed a law in Israel, which He* **commanded our fathers, That t***hey should make them known to their children**; That* **the generation to come** *might know them, the children who would be born, that* **they may arise and declare them to their children**, *That they may set their hope in God, and not forget the works of God, but keep His commandments."*

This is the perfect picture of how God originally planned for faith to be passed on generationally–not by the prophets themselves, not by the local church pastors of today. God intended for parents to be the primary faith seed-sowers in the life of their children, to create a multigenerational cycle of faith transference.

Before we move on, let's consider a few other passages of Scripture that reinforce God's desire for parents to be their children's primary spiritual leaders.

In John 15:1-17, Jesus says that He is the vine and we are the branches that bear fruit when we are connected to Him. He also points out that the Father prunes the branches so that they will become even more fruitful. I love this picture of God the Father as the gardener who tends closely to the branches on the vine. It gives us great insight into the role of the parent. We are to pay close attention to our children, pruning, shaping, helping them to bear fruit. Ensuring they stay connected to the vine of Christ. And just as the Father is glorified in the fruit we produce, I believe parents are blessed and honored when their children remain in the Lord and continue following Jesus all the days of their life.

In Ephesians 6:4, fathers are instructed to bring up their children in discipline and instruction of the Lord. "Bring up" in Greek means "to nourish up to maturity." God's design is for parents to help their children grow and mature through discipleship in the ways of God. As Proverbs 22:6 says, the hope-filled result of this intentional work is that their children will stay true to their faith throughout their lives.

In Proverbs 1:8-9, we see the imperative role of a parent under the section about resisting pressure from others to sin. "Hear, my son, your father's instruction, and forsake not your mother's teaching, for they are a graceful garland for your head and pendants for your neck" (ESV). Think about the value of a precious diamond necklace–and the status it implies in society. When someone wears priceless jewels, they instantly garner respect, even awe. This Scripture reveals the incredible value of the spiritual guidance of parents. It is priceless. We need to encourage our students to see the value of their parents' instruction and to regularly seek it out. And we need to reinforce to parents that their intentionality to teach their children the ways of God has greater worth than they know.

We see again and again in Scripture the significance of parents in the life of a child. While God surely can use ministry leaders like you and I to influence the lives of students, it is hard to overlook God's intention for the parent-child relationship, all the way to our own relationships with Him, our Father. He is the greatest source of wisdom and direction for our lives.

Chapter 3:
The Example of the Early Church

The president of Barna, David Kinnaman, published a book in 2011, called *You Lost Me*, that revealed 59% of young adults with a Christian background were dropping out of church at some point during their 20's–many for just a time, but some for good. Then, in 2019, he released another book called *Faith for Exiles: 5 Ways for a New Generation to Follow Jesus in a Digital Babylon*, in which he shared that the church dropout problem has not only remained an issue, but has increased over time from 59% to 64%, that nearly two-thirds of 18-29 year-olds in the U.S. who have grown up in church have withdrawn from church involvement. I believe that one of the greatest reasons for these discouraging statistics is that over the years, the western Church has positioned itself to be the main source for spiritual discipleship into the lives of students.

The early Church operated quite differently than it operates today. Smaller house churches were the setting of worship, teaching, fellowship and discipleship. Parents were next to their children the whole time. I'm not necessarily suggesting we revert back to this exact model, but I believe there is something wonderful to be learned from those who came before us. In these smaller church settings, children were powerfully impacted by being in close proximity to their parents, in a way that most kids and teens don't experience today.

The first reason for this is children got to see their parents practice their faith. They witnessed their parents modeling worship, stewardship of the Word, obedience in tithes and generous giving, and engagement in fellowship. Some of my favorite moments being a dad have taken place in a church service, holding my oldest son Caleb, seeing him look up at me with my hand raised in response to worship…and then seeing his little hand lift. Or grabbing my three children early from the kids ministry so they could see their momma lead the final worship song of the service. Kneeling down next to them and explaining why we worship the Lord in song. *As a parent responds to the gospel, a child can be led to do the same.*

Secondly, in the early Church, as families gathered together in one place, parents were consistently reminded of their responsibility to be the primary spiritual leader in their children's lives. Think about it: Today, parents drop their kids off in the kids' ministry or youth service on Sundays and don't see them until after service is dismissed. They're disconnected from their child's spiritual growth: out of sight, out of mind. I remember seeing my friend Cody during a worship night at our church; he had chosen to have his five year old with him in the service. Cody walked to the altar and knelt down on his knees. Soon after, Cody's son made his way down the aisle and mimicked his father's posture. I began to cry as I watched Cody lean over and teach his son why their posture in worship mattered so much to God. Not only did it make me wish my son Caleb was by my side, it made me emotional because I saw right before my eyes why ParentEquip matters. *When kids are close to their parents in spiritual settings, we, as parents, are reminded of our responsibility to raise them up in the Lord.* Let me ask you a question: When was the last time you or your pastor preached about parents' spiritual role in the lives of their children? If you can think of a recent time, look back even further. How often is this taught in your church? I would guess it doesn't happen often, or not often enough. This was a regular topic of discussion for the early Church. It should be the same for us today.

Thirdly, parents taught their children submission through their own submission to spiritual leadership. Today, even if parents are submitting to spiritual leadership, it is almost always in worship services for adults, through serving on a volunteer team, or in Small Groups…and if they aren't led to talk about these things with their kids outside of church, their children miss it entirely. Part of me wonders if the reason so many young people refuse to obey their parents is because they don't see their parents modeling obedience themselves. When I got married over ten years ago, I remember joking at the grocery store with my wife,"It's the best thing in the world to be married and out of the house, because I get to choose whatever cereal I want!" (This is actually far from the truth, because my wife rarely allows me to get Fruity Pebbles now like I did in the good ole days.) But think about it: Kids always want to be adults, because adults make their own rules, do what they want, and don't have to answer to anyone. Children who grow up seeing their parents submit to spiritual leadership could potentially see this entirely differently! I believe giving parents more regular opportunities to live out spiritual discipline and submission in front of their children is a key to changing a generation that currently believes they do not answer to anyone but themselves. This powerful parental example can flip the script!

I believe there are some specific reasons why the Church today has slowly drifted from the original model of the early Church. Some are likely just a response to the naturally ever-changing world we are living in. Others, though, are the result of shifting our focus to temporary ministry fruit that makes us feel we are doing better than we actually are. Let's take a look at a few of these reasons why we've drifted away from the original model.

Because so many pastors today are focused on growing a ministry numerically, they often make decisions that promote numbers at the expense of prioritizing discipleship. For instance, a pastor might spend months of time and hundreds of paid staff hours planning their next big evangelistic series where their church will see numerical growth but put little to no hours toward gaining, training and retaining new small group leaders. It's a "go get your friends" culture that does not have an adequate place for those friends to then grow in a smaller discipleship setting. We are losing sight of the big, long-term picture. While evangelism is absolutely biblical and important, discipleship is just as essential.

I've heard it said that we are living in the "microwave generation;" we want things to happen as fast as possible. And it takes a significant amount of planning and effort to disciple leaders who will then be capable and responsible for discipling students as small group leaders. The process of discipleship is slow, messy, exhausting, and certainly not as glamorous or "sexy" as the rapid growth we can see from our evangelistic efforts. So, it feels counter-intuitive to lean into the process of discipleship; it's difficult for us to structure our ministries around this long-term strategy. But we can't forget that the best things in life are developed over time, that the most impactful, long-lasting results come from an abundance of effort and investment.

We want things to move quickly in our ministries, for growth to be exciting and immediate, but we have to remember that Jesus spent 30 years with the Father in preparation for His three years of ministry! Why? So He would be ready to fulfill every bit of purpose intended for His life on earth. Discipleship is a slow, delicate process that requires focused attention, but if we are willing to see it through, we can see students living out their purpose in faithful, powerful service to God for their entire lives. We just can't rush it.

About six years ago, I experienced what I think is perhaps the single most defining moment of my ministry life. I was serving on staff at a megachurch that did an absolutely brilliant job drawing people in. One Sunday at the beginning of spring, we launched a new semester of small groups. It was our quarterly "Connection Group Weekend," where we kicked off over 150 small groups across all of our campuses. We had a super cool, excellently designed Connection Group Magazine that had a picture of each leader and a description of the group they were leading.

That weekend, two of our newest youth leaders walked up to me in our church lobby with a magazine in hand. They were teachers in a local high school that was a big target school for our youth ministry, and it was a huge blessing to have them on our volunteer team. The husband asked me if there were any men's discipleship groups or Bible studies available that semester, and I immediately responded with a confident, "Yes, of course, bro! Let me help." With over 150 groups launching, it seemed obvious to me that there would be a few options for him to choose from. But after flipping through the entire magazine, I realized why he had asked: There was not a single men's Bible study group. I was caught completely off guard. Of course, I did the whole stereotypical "confident-leader" response and said, "We must be missing something! Let me talk with our campus leadership, and I'll get back with you as soon as I have an answer." But even then, the answer remained, "We do not have any men's Bible study groups available."

I was sad and honestly really uncomfortable to give him the news. We had these two amazing, new leaders in our church who were looking to grow in their own personal discipleship as they were stepping up to disciple students… but there was nothing for them. Our church was great at attracting attendees, but at the end of the day, we were not creating an environment in which they could grow long term. I truly believe that prioritizing numerical growth undermines the discipleship of the congregation.

Another reason we've drifted from the original model of the early church is that our current church structures lead parents to subconsciously believe that youth and kids' ministries are the main contributor for spiritual development for their kids. They "drop their kids off" in a place where they will be discipled. Think about the language we often use in church: "We have amazing volunteers ready to care for your children and teach them about Jesus so you can enjoy church in a distraction-free environment." This implies two detrimental ideas: one, that the work of their children's discipleship is being taken care of by volunteers, and two, that children are a distraction that inhibits their own spiritual growth. We have to change our messaging!

Thinking back to Covid days and quarantine, as we engaged with church online, I realized how much I had adopted these detrimental ideas myself. I'll be the first to admit that I *really* missed Kids' Ministry–ha! We have three kids, and during that season, they were all under the age of five. When our "church-at-home" service was playing, my stress levels were over-the-top high! I'm a little embarrassed to say I yelled more during times of worship than I would like to admit. We would be singing "Peace Be Still," and I was yelling, "PLEASE BE STILL!" (Sorry, Dad joke...) I was so frustrated that I couldn't "focus" on church.

While my appreciation for kids' ministry grew during this time, so did my awareness of the flawed view I had of my responsibility as a parent. I was so focused on my own church experience that I lost track of the incredible ministry opportunity that was right before me: my littles. Over time, I began to let up on my extreme expectations of getting through a full at-home service peacefully and tried venturing out to find ways to engage them spiritually on our unique Sunday mornings. I was also reminded during that time that spiritual development doesn't just happen on Sunday morning; it happens multiple times a day. What an important realization, privilege, and joy! God really used our quarantine season to make me rethink my role in my children's spiritual development. I'm so grateful for the way He brought me back to the heart of the early Church.

If we as church leaders perpetuate a mental separation between parenting and discipling their children, we're essentially letting parents "off the hook" when it comes to spiritual leadership in their homes. And they won't push back on it–letting someone else disciple their child is certainly the easier route; being the primary spiritual leader can be tedious and difficult! We have to encourage parents to embrace the challenges that come with spiritual leadership and equip them for the job. I truly believe getting this messaging and approach to spiritual leadership right is essential for families to thrive in our churches. Our chosen ministry strategy will either resuscitate a parent's spiritual role in the life of their child or replace that God-designed role.

Let me reiterate: I am not against kids and youth ministries. I am absolutely for them! I am just for leveraging their ministry to impact the *family unit*, not just the child. One of the things I absolutely love about the kids ministry staff at my church is their regular effort to equip parents to lead in the home. I'll go over more of the practical things they do in Part 2 of this book, but part of their approach includes simple things like weekly resourcing emails and regular take-home materials provided at pick-up with follow-up challenges for parents to continue the conversation their kids were having in church, at home. There are many small, simple steps you can take in your ministry to begin helping parents step back into their God-designed role as spiritual leaders!

Another reason the Church has shifted from the model of the early church is that as the amount of disengaged and absent parents has increased, church leaders have felt responsible to fill in for parents, replacing parental spiritual discipleship entirely. Instead of responding to this absentee-parent reality with a greater effort to engage parents, we have stepped into their role. In my early years as a youth pastor, I remember celebrating the salvation of students who came into our ministry with totally lost parents, and eventually, the students' attendance in our church led their parents to begin attending. Some of their parents even began following Jesus! Of course, this is incredible! But while I loved these stories of families made whole again, over time, I became burdened by the abundance of young people being saved before their parents. God's original design was for this order to be flipped! The early Church demonstrated that parents were supposed to lead their children, not the other way around.

Some would say that this dynamic with disengaged parents will never change, but I plead with you not to give in to that belief. Of course, I still to this day passionately share the Gospel with students with unchurched parents, but I now put extra effort into engaging with their parents. I believe we can begin to see parents once again setting the *example* for discipleship and leading their kids to Christ, but it will require us to invest into parents in a whole new way. We have to believe this is possible and be willing to put in the work. Leaders see the ideal and build their efforts around accomplishing that ideal. We are not to accept this current, unfortunate reality of absentee parents and allow it to be standard. Let me try and convince you of something right now: What you're doing with your ministry today is either reinforcing parental disengagement or promoting the ideal. And the value we place on parental involvement is being communicated to our students. Students are watching us either call their parents to God's standard or letting them off the hook.

    I recently met with a father who was really struggling with some issues with his 16-year-old son. He wondered how things had gotten so bad. But from what I observed, I believe Mom and Dad played a decent part in their son's issues. Dad shared with me that his son had a big problem with anger and significantly lacked honor and submission to his parents. After talking with Dad, I could see how much this was weighing on them, so I sat with the son a couple weeks later to check in and see how things were going at home. He didn't reveal anything close to what his father had shared with me just days prior, which made me think that I needed to meet with them together. When I was able to get both father and son in the room, things began to come out in the open: honest emotions, hurts, broken trust, and the son's lack of desire to submit to his parents. But I also saw that Dad was not stepping up to lead his son as Scripture instructs us. This was my opportunity to begin bridging the gap between this father and his son.

    Throughout the conversation, I took little notes on a sticky note of words that stuck out to me that I felt spoke to deeper issues within this broken relationship. I eventually asked the son why he thought his dad was expecting a lot of him. After several minutes of the 16-year-old trying to identify the reason, I stood up and walked over to a large sticky note I had hanging on the back of my office door. (Yes, I'm a sticky note guy.) I wrote out the words *"because he cares"* in bold letters. Then, I looked at the son and asked, "Do you believe your dad cares about you?" He responded with a quick "yes." Then, I asked him why he thought his dad was so strict. He didn't have a very confident answer, so I turned to the dad and suggested, "Would you say that the main reason why you might be a little overbearing at times is because you want your son to have what you didn't and to refrain from making the same mistakes you made?" The dad dropped his head, almost in tears.

I turned back to the son to bring the truth home. "While your dad isn't perfect and makes mistakes, you have to remember his deeper heart. Your dad loves you, cares for you more than you can understand, and is afraid of you not having the life he believes you could have." I also made sure to speak to the dad in front of his son about his role as a father and as primary spiritual leader. I addressed his anger problem and how it wasn't a good example for his children. I also shared that because of the relational divide between him and his son, discipline would continue to be an almost impossible thing–that if he wanted his son to respond better to his rebukes and direction, he needed to lean in relationally more than ever before. By the end of this talk, both father and son were beginning to see their situation differently.

This conversation gave me the opportunity to really help *both of them* understand the idea of the spiritual authority of a parent. I reminded the teen, who was actually one of the most influential students in our ministry, that it's not honoring to God for him to be obedient at church with our youth team but rebellious and disrespectful at home. He needed to hear from me, as his pastor, that his father and mother are God's desired way to raise him up in the ways of the Lord. If he chose to see the worst in his parents and continued to resist their leadership, he would miss out on all the rich and important lessons they could be teaching him.

So how did this situation resolve? The father and son are still working on their relationship. It's not perfect, but they're making progress. Now, every time I see the parents or their son, I continue to emphasize the parents' role as the primary spiritual leader. I remind the student that God didn't make a mistake by making them his parents. It takes work and repetition, but I believe this emphasis and proper reordering of spiritual authority is making a big difference in their family. If we embrace this work, I believe we can begin to emulate the early Church and see the kind of generational fruit they saw in the beginning–fruit that changed the world and built a body of believers that has lasted for over 2,000 years.

Chapter 4:
God's Design for Families

I remember going to a Promise Keepers event with my dad two decades ago. If you've never heard of Promise Keepers, just picture a massive weekend conference where tens of thousands of men, from all different walks of life, come together to worship, gather in groups and are challenged to live a life of integrity. I will never forget that particular weekend for two specific reasons. The first is because it was the first time I ever saw my dad weep like a child–and I mean, *weep*. He was so touched, challenged, and impacted that he was moved to heavy emotion multiple times. The second reason I will never forget that event is that watching my dad respond emotionally caused me to respond emotionally myself. At first, it felt so uncomfortable, crying there in my father's arms. I felt embarrassed. Unsure. Vulnerable. But it quickly turned into a bonding moment with him that twenty years later still brings tears to my eyes.

One of the moments that really touched my dad emotionally was when the worship team began to lead "It Is Well," and thousands of passionate voices filled the arena. "It Is Well" was my Papa's favorite song, and he had passed away not long before that event. My dad's breath was taken away, remembering his father; he folded over like he had been punched in the gut as he was hit by grief and gratitude for the impact his dad had had on his life. My grandfather's spiritual legacy was passed from my grandfather to my dad to me. Seeing my dad respond with emotional vulnerability in the presence of God influenced me to follow suit.

There is no doubt that we do a lot of good, meaningful, impactful work in next generation ministry. But moments like this, when a child is led by their parents' example in following God, will always be the most significant and long-lasting ones. Parents will always have greater influence and impact potential than we could ever have through church. Why? *Because this is God's design.*

I recognize that a good percentage of students in our ministries do not have parents who are believers. You may be thinking, *"We can't expect a parent who does not believe in Christ to be the primary spiritual leader."* While this is absolutely true, I want to note that numerous psychological studies have shown that protective factors in a child's life are directly associated with healthy attachment and connection to their parents. So, while the parent may not be able to provide spiritual direction for a specific season, their presence and engagement in their children's lives is still incredibly important. God designed the relationship between child and parent to be not only spiritual but emotional, psychological, and physical as well. I mention this because our attitude toward parents, whether they believe in Jesus or not, has to be positive and supportive. We have to believe that God knew what He was doing when He designed the family unit and support families in every way we can.

The fact that many parents are not Christ-followers often becomes an argument for not engaging and equipping parents in next generation ministry. We are missing so many opportunities if we adopt this as our philosophy. We miss the opportunity to reach parents with the truth of the Gospel, and we overlook our ability to help strengthen the families we serve.

While this demographic of parents can add some complexity to an equipping strategy, it shouldn't determine our overall belief about the spiritual role of a parent in a child's life. Regardless of the spiritual status of the parent, God's design for families does not change.

Whenever God's design is altered, we will most certainly see grave consequences. I truly believe parents being disengaged, unequipped, or unbelieving is largely due to the Church not creating a ministry strategy that positions parents to lead. When we broaden our perspective as next generation pastors to see the most fruitful ministry being to families, we will begin to see an increase of parents growing as disciples. I believe this shift can change the trajectory of a generation.

ParentEquip may be the most important thing you begin to implement in your ministry over the course of this next year. I realize that you may not feel you need to make changes if you're seeing some great visible fruit of ministry. If you're seeing incredible numbers of salvations, baptisms, booming small groups, and epic "invite events/series" with consistent broken attendance records, you may wonder why you would do anything differently. "If it ain't broke, don't fix it," right?

I think we need to recognize what kind of ministry is most fruitful long term. Over the past couple decades, ministries have focused on and celebrated growing attendance, centering their fundamental ministry models around gatherings and larger events. And while many of us may say we prioritize discipleship, our programming and priorities don't always align with that declaration. Let me give you an example: If you had followed me around when I was a young youth pastor, you would have been quite proud of my vision-casting abilities (ha). I had these nice, pretty vision statements that I'd repeat all the time to our students and to our leaders. One of those statements was, "We are a youth ministry that prioritizes small groups." Sounds great, right? Well, the leaders who served on my team and oversaw our small groups heard me say that all the time, but they also watched me consistently preach 25 extra minutes into our small group time. And they rightly began to question if my vision statement was truly accurate. From many conversations over the years, I'm confident I'm not the only next gen pastor who has ever had a clear vision (and truly believed it!) but made choices that did not support that vision.

Most of us have great philosophies and spend hours, days, even months at a time planning and dreaming about future plans for our ministry, but we rarely, if ever, ask, "How will we impact the *home* with our ministry?" I've come to believe this is a devastating oversight. It's a disservice to the family unit, and I believe that it's ultimately dishonoring to God. After a couple decades celebrating record church attendance across the board, we are still seeing large percentages of graduates walk away from their faith.

If anything, we are seeing even more renounce their faith than before, even though ministries have become steadily bigger, grander and more attractive. It's time to shift our focus from the fruit that's immediate and exciting to the fruit that lasts.

When I was a youth pastor in Florida, there was a girl in my ministry who, when she first began attending, was as sketchy as it comes. Jess was the type of student that would push limits, just to see how much she could get away with before getting into trouble. One time, she walked up to me and said, "Pastor Sam, what would you do if I told you I had cocaine on me?" I told her I would have her arrested if she didn't flush it down the toilet. (Ha!) My head of security, who was high up in our local sheriff's department, was standing right next to me. I looked at this 15-year-old and, pointing to my friend, said, "This will be the guy who arrests you."

Fast-forward a few months, and I began seeing the Lord do some incredible work in her life. Jess went from being the definition of trouble to applying for our student leadership team. I remember her cussing me out during our internship workouts because she didn't want to run…she was still a work in process, for sure. But over time, she began to flourish. She trusted the Lord with her life and began to serve faithfully. Eventually, she did become one of the team leads in our ministry. It was incredible to watch her be transformed by the love of God. I remember vividly the Lord speaking to me about a pastoral call on her life. Seeing where she came from, it was truly a miracle: God at work.

But though I was watching Jess grow spiritually at church, I wasn't really paying attention to what was going on at home. Jess, in her rebellion, displayed some characteristics of a broken home, but I was too young in my leadership to draw the correlation between the two. Today, when I see a troubled student, I look past their apparent issues for a moment to begin identifying what their home life looks like, what their background is. I know this isn't always the root of a student's issues; many troubled kids do have remarkable parents. But for a large majority, rebellious kids return from church to brokenness at home. This was Jess' reality, but I missed it. Over time, I began to see that with every two steps forward she made at church, she was taking three backwards at home. Her parents were alcoholics; her dad had an anger problem; both parents showed massive favoritism to Jess' younger sister. Jess always felt less-than and overlooked. It began to make sense why she struggled with a variety of things for so long and why it was so very difficult for her to remain free.

If I had known then what I know now, I would have handled things quite differently. After I transitioned out of my role at that church, I saw from afar that Jess fell away from her faith. She had a great small group leader and had strong church community, but the impact of her home life was in many ways too tough for her to overcome. I wonder what things would look like today for Jess if I spent more time with her parents, if I had been more intentional to connect them to the Gospel and help them connect relationally to their daughter. Based on what I've seen over the years as I've implemented the ParentEquip strategy, things really could have looked different.

Sadly, I have multiple stories like this. I bet you do as well. The truth is, quite often our ministry efforts can be hindered by a broken home. The question I'm posing to you is: What if, instead of working hard to help students follow Jesus through our ministry alone, we can see the significance of the role parents play in that process and invest energy there as well? Yes, not all parents are in a position to disciple and embody that primary spiritual leader role, but what if your ministry could not only be responsible for young people following God's call for their life, but helping restore the whole family unit to its original, God-given design?

Parents don't always know *how* to lead their child spiritually. They may not be disengaged and/or absent; they may very well want to help grow their child spiritually! But many simply don't know how. Additionally, some parents may not know how to lead their child spiritually because their own discipleship journey is immature and in need of development. The ParentEquip strategy does not require you to take on this complete discipleship process. Hopefully your church is already actively discipling adults and helping them grow! But I will suggest, however, that we should take some responsibility specifically in next gen ministry to help parents grow. We should find it an absolute joy to encourage and equip parents to disciple their children. We have to remember that a parent cannot invest into their child what they do not have for themself. Parents do need help, and this is the foundation of ParentEquip.

By embracing and implementing the ParentEquip model in our next generation ministries, we are partnering with God in His very purposeful design for families: that through parental discipleship, children develop a solid, unshakable faith, strengthened within their family unit. The crux of it is empowering parents to step into their role of spiritual leadership rather than replacing them with church leadership. When we connect parents to their God-given roles, I believe we do a few very important things:

1. We position the family unit to function as it was designed by God, thus inviting the blessing of God onto the family.
2. We help restore intimacy between a child and their parents.
3. We help parents become the heroes in their kids' lives, allowing them to win and be relationally connected with their child in a way that can bless the rest of their lives and generations to come.
4. We help promote an atmosphere in families in which students can develop deeply-rooted faith that will endure throughout their lives.

God's original design IS best, and if we can take steps to return to His plan for families and discipleship, where the primary space for growth is in the home, facilitated by parents, I believe we will begin to see a shift in the next generation. Local churches are powerful and will never be irrelevant, but our work will be that much more powerful when we realign with God's incredible design, working together with parents to raise children up in the Lord. Let's embrace this plan and begin to make changes!

In the following chapters, you will see the three foundations of the ParentEquip strategy. Each of these three foundations is multi-faceted, but let me encourage you not to get overwhelmed. The goal is to begin taking small steps in each area, and the first step is simply to adopt what I would call a "parent filter." You can do this by consistently asking, *"How can we leverage this to equip parents to lead spiritually?"* in every area of your ministry.

Before we dive into the ParentEquip strategy, I want to make a few important notes to help you set realistic expectations.

1. The ParentEquip strategy requires you to hold loosely to your current ministry philosophy. Please know that I have incredible respect for you as a ministry leader but also allow me to be honest: Some of what you're doing right now might not be producing as much longterm fruit as you think. As I mentioned before, I believe many ministries think they are more successful than they really are because of the temporal fruit their events and strategies are creating. I will probably challenge some of the ways you currently think about next generation ministry; please be ok with that. For years, I have heard from brilliant leadership minds that "the best idea wins." To embrace this truth, we have to be willing to let go of some long-held beliefs about strategy and learn a new way to accomplish our vision, which of course will remain the same. As Andy Stanley says, "Marry the mission; date the model."

2. The ParentEquip strategy requires us to develop a passion and love for parents, not just their kids! If you were to ask my staff who I love spending the most time with, they would all laugh knowingly and then immediately say, "Parents." This doesn't mean I don't like spending my time with students; I abso-

lutely enjoy hanging with the students in our ministry! Whether it's slamming some Chipotle with the football team, playing 3v3 basketball before service, or trying hard to compete with the legendary Super Smash Bro players in our video game area, I still find great joy in tangible moments with students. Time with young people allows me to stay connected to the everyday life of kids and youth. It positions me to remain effective in my ministry as a youth pastor. I deeply believe, however, that without engaging parents with the purpose of equipping and empowering them to lead spiritually, my ministry effectiveness is *limited*. I would propose the same is true for you.

When I talk to next generation leaders, I often hear them say they don't feel comfortable around parents. Just recently, I was on a coaching call with a large multisite church and the next gen pastor shared with me beforehand that part of why he asked me to coach his team was that a lot of his younger leaders lacked confidence with parents. I've found a few reasons why a next gen leader might struggle in this area:

- ◆ The leader may be young (or not yet a parent) and feel as if they don't have much to offer someone who has been parenting for many years.
- ◆ The leader may think that because the parents have fallen incredibly short or have a track record of not showing up, they, as the leader, are

now responsible for picking up the slack. This thought can cause leaders to become bitter with parents, which consequently affects their interactions and beliefs about parental authority in the lives of their students.

◆ The leader may not see parents as part of their ministry focus. Simply put, "They are why we have weekend services." While we do, of course, design weekend services to serve the adults of our congregation, this way of thinking is founded on the assumption that parents and their kids are separate and have separate spiritual lives. That is simply not the case. That is not God's original design for discipleship. He has always intended for the family unit to grow in Him together. If we are in kids' ministry or youth ministry, we are in the ministry of families.

3. As we go through this process, many of us may need to mourn the fact that some of what we've done in ministry has not been as effective as we thought it was. This has been a tough part of my own journey as I have developed ParentEquip. Looking back on past ministry efforts, while great things did happen, I can see now that I missed the mark at producing long-lasting fruit in the family unit. Many of the students I might have considered my "greatest ministry success stories" over the years have gone away from the faith, and that might not have been the case if I hadn't missed the steps discussed in this book. These are painful realities to face, but I believe we will all be

much better for it. Our willingness to confront our shortcomings and make adjustments will bless the lives of our students and families in profound ways. The ParentEquip strategy requires a "long game" perspective. This strategy was not designed with the goal to make your ministry grow quickly, so don't go in with the expectation that you'll "explode" numerically once you apply these principles. If you do, you'll miss the whole heart and core motivation behind ParentEquip. If we are to "reinstate" parents as the primary spiritual leaders in their kids' lives, it will require us to take a bit of a backseat in the heroism of ministry. ParentEquip is about shifting students from seeing us as the heroes to seeing their parents as the heroes.

When you think of "heroes in the faith," who do you think of? Certainly many think of Moses, David, the Apostles. Maybe you think of remarkable theologians, evangelists, or preachers who have left an inspiring mark on this world. I could easily say my pastor, Kevin Taylor, is a hero in the faith. Or his predecessor, Dan Remus. One of the pastors I served years ago, Derek Williams, would for sure be on my list as well. Early in our marriage, my wife and I saw a counselor named Mike Lowery, and to us, he was the definition of a hero. I could go on and on. Over the years I have heard so many people share about their personal "heroes in the faith." But I have always been most inspired when people name a parent as their hero. Could you imagine if the kids and teens that make up your ministry called their parents their heroes? What if, one day, the 16-year-old son I mentioned earlier could see his dad as a "hero in the faith" in his journey walking with Jesus? My prayer is that as you read the rest of this book, you will be inspired and become passionate about equipping parents to be the heroes in the faith of their child's story.

So let us not delay any longer! Here is ParentEquip.

Part Two: The Strategy

Chapter 5: (Foundation #1)

Community
----(over)----
Communication

The first foundation of ParentEquip is a new perspective on the idea of communication. Many of us put a great deal of thought into what we communicate by how we speak or the kinds of emails we send out, and while that is a vital aspect of communication in the life of a church, I believe it's missing an essential second half–literally! This kind of outward-bound communication tends to be almost entirely one-sided. We inform church members and parents about events. We "keep them in the loop." But this honestly does nothing to really build relationship with the people with whom we are communicating, which leaves our work as pastors and leaders incomplete. Certainly, if this one-way communication is the extent to which we involve parents in next generation ministry, we are missing the boat entirely.

While keeping parents updated with ministry information is, of course, important, one-way communication reinforces the perception that our ministry is in charge of their children's spiritual lives: We are the ones doing the organizing and planning; we are determining memory verses and curriculum; there's really no need for them to do much of anything. If we want parents to step into their God-given roles as the primary spiritual leaders in the lives of their children, we need to change this perception–and our communication strategy plays a big role in that effort.

The crux of the ParentEquip strategy is cultivating dialogue with parents and subsequently empowering parents to dialogue with their children. This requires us to focus on community and connection with parents, which we can only build through *back-and-forth* communication and open discussion. Communication without "community" leaves parents on the outside looking in, somewhat aware of but disengaged from the spiritual discipleship of their children. But if we can build a community that really involves parents and facilitates active discussion, we can help them re-engage in their roles as spiritual leaders in a powerful way.

I believe the kind of dialogue we want to cultivate with parents is multifaceted. I see four particularly important lines of communication that we need to facilitate:

Ministry Leader to Parent
Parent to Ministry Leader
Parent to Parent
Small Group Leader to Parent

The "community" vision of the ParentEquip strategy requires all four of these lines of communication to be open and active. If one is missing, we miss out on the benefits of a truly holistic Next Generation community. Let's take a look at the philosophy behind engaging each of these lines of communication, their specific benefits, and the practical steps we can take to establish them.

Ministry Leader-to-Parent Communication

Excellent communication from ministry leaders to parents is absolutely essential for cultivating community. Of the four lines of communication discussed in this chapter, I think this is the one most next generation ministries already utilize, though there may be more effective ways to do so. One of the mistakes we often make in our ministry leader-to-parent communication is not sharing *enough* information–or not doing so in a timely fashion. Over the years as a next gen leader, I've learned that the fastest way to create a group of frustrated parents is to communicate poorly and change things last minute. This chips away at the idea of community in a couple different ways: Of course, it's annoying to a parent to feel like they don't really know what's going on, but it also erodes the sense of trust if parents consistently feel out of the loop or surprised by last-minute plans. If we want to cultivate community with parents and help them engage with our ministry and students, we need to provide **ample** information *with time to spare*! **Over-communication** is the first step to growing a supportive, involved group of parents in your ministry.

One of my favorite ways to do this is to invite parents to be a part of building momentum for events, especially when we have something big on the horizon. We did this recently during our annual "Winter Camp Live" event, where all of our campuses join together for an event that's entirely focused on our upcoming Winter Camp. Winter Camp Live is a highly strategic night, because we have a chance to give both students and parents a glimpse into camp life: We worship with our camp band, play some of our camp games, and hear a short message from our camp speaker. We hold this event four weeks before the beginning of camp and coordinate it to be the final night of camp registration.

I can't tell you what a win it is to have all of the parents from our community join us for a night like this. It builds excitement that parents can share with their kids and also establishes a real sense that we are *doing this together*. This year, we saw our highest parent attendance since I joined the staff, and it got me so FIRED UP! As I walked around that night, shaking hands and giving hugs, I was able to thank the parents for joining us and tell them how much I cared that they were there. It gave me the opportunity to really reinforce the fact that we want them to be involved in what we're doing as a ministry.

Cultivating a belief within a parent that they should play a part and that you, as a leader, value their involvement deeply is very important! I walked up to a particular mom and said, "Hey Cindy, thanks so much for joining us tonight. I cannot begin to explain how much it means to me." And she said, without skipping a beat, "Well, Pastor Sam, there's no way I could miss this night after receiving your 17th email!" I literally laughed out loud and then internally did the Napoleon Dynamite "yesss," arm and all. Did I really send seventeen emails? No. Did I come close to that over a period of two months...probably! I know it may feel a little uncomfortable to over-communicate with parents. You might worry that you'll overwhelm them or annoy them, and certainly there's something to be said for not sending 4 emails a day. But if the turnout for our Winter Camp Live event this year was any indication, parents **want** to know *all the things*. And they want to be invited to be a part!

Of course, parents can't always be physically present at youth camps and retreats, so we need to work to find other ways to help them feel connected and involved while their students are away. Utilizing a texting service like "Remind" allows us as ministry leaders to keep the line of communication open with parents throughout events. When parents register their students for conferences or camps, we provide a QR code or link with simple instructions to help parents opt in to our Parent Text for the weekend. The Parent Text will include photo updates throughout the event, quotes from small group leaders about moments of life change, main topics from the messages, epic game moments, reflections on the day...

This allows us to update parents *throughout* the camp/event experience so they can know what is happening during a significantly formative time for their child, in real time. While a parent isn't physically present, they can remain prayerfully engaged and still go on the journey with their child, in a way. Sharing ways their children are growing and connecting with the Lord can also spark new interest in their own spiritual growth. As we discussed earlier, some parents don't know they are supposed to be leading their child spiritually or, perhaps, don't currently have a desire to do so. By communicating with them and including them in powerful camp moments, you can help cultivate a desire to experience spiritually formative moments like that for themselves and to encourage their children to continue to pursue God once the event concludes.

Using a texting strategy to communicate with parents also allows students to be more present. Have you ever led a student camp or trip and had "that" parent (or many parents) who contacted their kid a dozen times a day? "Did you eat this morning?" "Did you get any sleep?" "Are you getting into trouble?" "Is your small group leader letting you share what's on your heart?" "Do you need me to bring you anything?" Or what about the famous, "Why didn't you text me before bed last night?" The student responds, "Mom, I was praying at the altar until after your normal bedtime." While they aren't intending to detract from their students' experience, parental interruptions can cause major distractions in the camp experience for their child. When we use this simple texting tool, we alleviate the urgency a parent might feel to reach out so much. I also encourage parents to contact me first if they need to connect with their children; this helps me communicate that there really are times when their child needs to be focused on what we're doing, in the moment, at the event. We can all work together to make sure our students have the best, most impactful experience.

It is so very important that we get the Ministry Leader-to-Parent Communication part of our ministry right; it sets the foundation for success for all the other lines of communication we'll talk through next. The quality of our communication to parents will determine whether or not they see us as reliable and trustworthy. Parental trust is the lifeblood of the community we are working to build through ParentEquip.

Parent-to-Ministry Leader Communication

I firmly believe this is one of the most important aspects of next generation ministry and maybe the most important form of communication in the "community" I'm encouraging you to build. When parents have access to you as the ministry leader, it's a doorway to begin bridging gaps between the parents and their kids. When we give parents the opportunity to connect with us personally, we facilitate a partnership of spiritual leadership that can, at some point, allow us as leaders to educate, equip and empower parents to be the primary leaders God designed them to be. The hope for focusing on this area of communication is to build the relational equity needed to really help disciple parents and one day hand spiritual leadership back to the parents.

In a coaching session with another youth pastor recently, I asked how accessible he thought he was to the parents in his youth ministry. He wasn't sure how to answer the question, so I led him with another: "How do you contact parents, and how do parents contact you?" He shared that he uses his office phone to call parents and asks parents to use that number if they need to get in touch with him. The advice I gave him next is what I'm about to share with you. And I know it's a bit controversial, but please hear me out: I believe if we really want to get this second line of communication right, *parents need our personal cell phone number*. Or, at the bare minimum, a Google Voice number…some way they can feel like they have direct access to us when they really need it. Options like Google Voice are better than nothing, but I want to stress that I believe sharing our personal mobile number is the best way to facilitate the kind of community we want to build. The moment you become ok with making yourself available to parents this way, your ability to equip and empower parents will grow exponentially.

Right now, our youth ministry "community" is made up of over 400 parents. We've worked hard to build this community for two years, and we've seen some pretty incredible fruit come from it. I know it might sound scary or crazy, but each of those 400 parents has access to my real cell phone number. Our ministry, now built on the ParentEquip strategy, holds it as a core value that parents have the ability to communicate directly with me and our Next Gen staff.

When I suggested this to the youth pastor I mentioned above, he immediately had reservations about giving out his phone number. And I get that. It feels vulnerable; there's a natural concern that they won't respect boundaries. His concerns were the same as many other next gen leaders: "What if they call me all the time?" "What if they call me at random hours of the night?" "Will I ever really be 'off duty' with my family?" These are, of course, valid concerns, but let me tell you that my experience with sharing my number has been nothing but positive. In the almost three years I've been at my church, I have had ZERO parents abuse my number. Zero parents have called too much, zero parents have shared my number with their kids, and zero parents have called me at a crazy time of the night outside of rare, very valid emergency situations that we all signed up for when we became next generation ministry leaders.

There are a few strategies that I want to share with you that have allowed our ministry to successfully set boundaries with this communication strategy, safeguarding the privacy of myself and our leaders while still giving them access to a spiritual leader partnership with us. The bottom line is that we have to be up front about what is acceptable and what is NOT acceptable, right from the beginning of our partnership. When I first share my contact information with parents, I say a few basic statements that help me establish firm boundaries from the beginning.

"Please do not call me and leave a voicemail. I rarely answer phone calls because of the amount of spam calls I receive. Text me, and I will respond much faster." - This allows me to set straight forward expectations for how they can most successfully get in touch with me, while leaving some room for light hearted jokes about spam calls… nine times out of ten the parent laughs and says, "Me too!" I think it also helps me build relational equity with them, because they get to know my communication style. The honesty of sharing, "I don't answer phone calls," actually helps rather than hinders.

"I am off on Fridays and Saturdays with my family. That does not mean you cannot contact me, but it does mean I might have a delayed response. Sometimes, I won't respond until Sunday." - This is my way of creating healthy boundaries for the sake of my family. This also helps us immediately take a step forward in "educating and equipping" parents. We set the example of prioritizing days of

rest and family time. One of the most significant causes of broken homes is a lack of prioritization of rest and family time. When parents see us doing this right in our own homes, they can follow our example as they step into their primary spiritual leadership role!

"If there is some sort of emergency with your student, call me three times in a row." - I will never forget a particular date night with my wife, Elizabeth, when I was a youth pastor in Florida. We were at the Gulf Coast Town Center mall, a pretty regular date night spot for us, and we were enjoying some great food. During our dinner, I received multiple phone calls to inform me that one of my students was actively talking about committing suicide. Knowing the student, their history and the relationship I had built with their parents, Elizabeth and I both knew that our date night was going to turn into a significant pastoral opportunity. We ended up spending the rest of the evening with this student, providing urgent pastoral care and support. These crisis situations are rare, but they are moments when parents need us and just need extra support. There are also definitely times that demand 911 calls or hospital visits. I didn't sign up to do what I do to leave parents hanging in their most difficult moments.

Times of crisis are *opportunities*–opportunities to **show up for a parent**, further cementing the foundational trust that empowers a spiritual leader partnership, in addition to supporting the student. I believe that parents reaching out to us during tough times is a sign that we're doing a good job partnering with them. They call us because they trust us. They might not know WHAT to do, but they know WHO to call. We can't take those moments for granted.

Another thing we can do to foster this parental partnership and support system is to encourage small group leaders to be available to parents in the same way. If we see parents reaching out to their children's small group leaders when going through something difficult, we are building a healthy parent community. This tangible marker is definitely a goal to shoot for! If you're still hesitating about giving parents your personal cell number, consider the fact that we want parents to be able to contact small group leaders directly. If we expect our leaders to give their number to parents, why wouldn't we do the same?

Let me illustrate the power of this Parent to Leader line of communication. Just a few weeks ago, a dad reached out to me regarding a situation his daughter experienced at our camp. Apparently, she shared some sensitive information with her small group at camp (HUGE WIN), but one of the girls in her group talked about it outside the group (HUGE WIN SQUASHED). Over the last few months, this has caused some tension in her small group; his daughter hasn't really wanted to return to church. It's been everything he can do to keep her engaged in church. His job is quite stressful, and his ex-wife is constantly trying to pull their daughter in a destructive direction, causing problems and creating tension in their family. He shared with me that he has recently felt close to a breaking point. On the phone the other day, he told me that over the last week, he has felt like a horrible father. He's lost his temper and hasn't been as supportive to his daughter the way he wants to. The shame and guilt from all of that was really weighing him down.

Have you ever talked to a parent who sounded downright defeated? If not, let me encourage you to talk to parents more! So many parents feel this way, and they need our support. Gratefully, even though the dad felt this way, he sure was talking to the right guy: I went into ParentEquip mode, a.k.a. "encourage the heck out of this dad and remind him of his calling as his daughter's spiritual leader."

I told him how encouraging it was for me to hear him wrestling with how he had fallen short, that it was admirable that he cared enough to recognize that he had dropped the ball. I also reminded him that he is one of, I don't know… a billion parents that have weeks like he just had. Instantly, I could hear his tone change, like his shoulders were relaxing for the first time in days. I then shared with him the power of connecting his faults to the spiritual growth of his daughter. I urged him to remember that while he is flawed, his daughter's heavenly Father isn't. I challenged him to sit and talk with her soon and even compare his flaws to God's perfection. As he acknowledged his mistakes, he could remind his daughter that because he is a flawed person, he will undoubtedly mess up and make mistakes—but God the Father, in His perfection, never will. This dad can lead her in that moment to lean on God when her parents fall short. Laying out this foundational spiritual principle for his daughter and humbly asking for her forgiveness would increase the level of trust in their relationship and open the door for him to lead her spiritually even more in the future.

This conversation never would have happened if that dad didn't feel he had permission to call me. Giving parents access to us helps us build relational equity and become true partners with them. And the equity we gain with parents, if stewarded well, will eventually lead to greater equity between the parents and their children. When we communicate without building a community, we say, *"This is what I'm doing,"* instead of *"This is what we can do together."* This is why we cannot just communicate TO the parent, we need to open up the line of communication from the parent to us! As parents become more accustomed to communicating openly with us, their hearts become open to the next level of Parent Community communication, which is Parent-to-Parent communication.

Parent-to-Parent Communication

Parenting is one of the most rewarding but challenging experiences people navigate in this life. It's a complete roller coaster, where you can go to bed feeling like a winner but feel like a failure before even leaving for work the next morning. Parents need encouragement more regularly than they admit, and they need more support than we can provide as ministry leaders. By cultivating parent-to-parent communication, you can support parents while also empowering them to operate as the body of Christ as they serve one another. And as they grow in their confidence to support one another, they will more boldly step into their roles as spiritual leaders in their own homes. Creating a safe space for parents to connect with other parents in similar seasons of life is incredibly beneficial for their family units, as well as your ministry community.

There are many ways to cultivate parent-to-parent communication, but here are two of the most effective I have found:

Parent Community Platform: Facebook Groups has been my go-to platform for building our parent community for years now. I will dive a bit deeper into the specifics on how to utilize a Facebook page to facilitate community later in this book, but for now, I'll say our ministry's Youth Parent Community group has become a place where parents encourage one another daily, answer questions before our staff can get to them, and help us spread the word about different details and events in our ministry. It may feel a little intimidating to empower parents to "lead" each other this way; I understand the concern about "overzealous" parents. But I believe you'll find the benefits far outweigh the inconvenience of that rare situation. Fostering this community communication allows our parents to be connected with each other, as well as feel like they're really a part of our ministry as a whole.

Parent Nights and Events: The more you can get parents in an intentional "face-to-face" environment with one another, the more you'll see the impact of this communication lane. Whether church-wide parent events, parent Zoom calls, or just an evening where you invite parents to shadow your ministry, there's great benefit in gathering parents together!

Parent-to-Parent communication creates space for a couple important things: Parents begin to associate themselves with other parents in their particular parenting season. This will naturally develop small support systems within your parent ministry, cultivating a culture of community and encouragement. As parents connect with one another, their families will become more integrated into your ministry as a whole. It becomes a beautiful group project of sorts, with parents figuring out together how to lead their children through difficult moments in life. This provides an increase of care for parents in the midst of crisis. As parents connect, they will rely on each other in difficult times! We can offer them limited support, but a strong parent community can rally around a family for as long as is needed.

A few months ago, we held one of our quarterly Parent Connect Nights, where we gather parents from across all of our campuses for an evening of connection and resourcing. At these events, we always work hard to place parents at round tables with other parents in similar seasons. On this night, I sat down at a table with a group of parents who all had kids between the ages of 2 and 5. You can imagine we all laughed quite a bit! We went back and forth, telling super sweet stories, as well as ones that would win us the grand prize on America's Funniest Home Videos. We shared lighthearted moments and also had deep conversations about the real struggles that come with parenting toddlers. It was amazing to experience the power of "me too" moments, when parents realized they weren't alone in their challenges. You could feel the sense of community support building right in that moment.

Parents become evangelistic and help the ministry grow. If parents become passionate about your ministry and have a healthy trust in your leadership, they will begin talking to their friends about it. We openly welcome parents to invite their parent friends to our Community platform on Facebook. Parents who don't even attend our church are a part of our Community. I attribute a great percentage of the growth we've experienced in this last season to this aspect of our communication strategy. We have not overtly asked students to invite friends to church lately, and we haven't really hosted any large events aside from our Winter Camp. I am confident that the growth we've seen is because of parents reaching out to other parents.

Just the other day, a parent who doesn't attend our church texted me. Her son recently attended one of our youth services with a friend who is a part of our ministry. This mom had gotten my number from a friend of hers in hopes of finding a way to register her son for summer camp. Their family can't afford camp, so she was reaching out to inquire about a scholarship so her son could attend. There are a couple things I love about this situation: First, I love that a parent in our ministry passed my number to a friend, knowing I would do my best to get their unchurched son into our camp. This shows the trust that mom has in me as a leader and in our ministry. As with anything else, word of mouth referrals are the greatest sign of a good reputation. Second, I love having the opportunity to help this other mom feel seen and heard as we work to accommodate her request for financial assistance, even before she has set foot in our church. As we've operated in the ParentEquip strategy over the past few years, I've seen many new families join the church because they felt prioritized and cared for before they'd even started attending. I believe that as we partner with this new mom and help her son attend camp, she will grow to trust us and eventually share about our ministry with others, just as her friend shared with her.

When we foster parent-to-parent communication and help parents feel like they're a part of our ministries, our impact extends beyond the ministries themselves and into the neighborhoods that surround our churches.

Small Group Leader-to-Parent Communication

As ministry leaders, we cannot be the only ones who embrace and embody the ParentEquip strategy; our volunteers must do so as well. Volunteers, especially those serving as small group leaders, have to shift their thinking, just like we do, from only seeing and serving students to seeing and serving parents as well. We need to help our small group leaders grasp the vision to empower parents to be the primary leaders.

We can facilitate a greater sense of community and support among parents when we train our small group leaders to engage with and be available to parents. Every parent is walking through something with their child, and as ministry leaders, there's no way we can minister to every single one. We have to empower the next tier of leadership in our ministry to provide pastoral care and further equip parents to step into their roles as their children's primary spiritual leaders. If this is our mission, we have to gain, train and retain amazing leaders who help make the mission a reality.

As the ministry leader, you'll be responsible for setting expectations for your volunteers to build relationships with parents and creating regular opportunities for your small group leaders to connect with parents. Here are a few examples of ways we create these opportunities in our ministry:

1. Whenever we launch a new semester of youth small groups, we ensure our small group schedule has built-in-time for parents to meet their child›s small group leader before the group. I specifically instruct our small group leaders to go out of their way to

meet and exchange contact info with their students' parents.

2. Whenever we do parent nights (where we train parents and help them connect with one another), we do our best to have small group leaders in the room to reinforce that personal connection.

3. We encourage small group leaders to text and connect with parents on a regular basis.

4. For larger youth events like camps and retreats, we are intentional about creating space where parents and leaders can connect. We have found hosting pre-camp parent meetings that take place a week or two before camp is a fantastic way to unite small group leaders with parents. These meetings give leaders the opportunity to share their contact info with parents, and the parents can express any thoughts or concerns they might have about their children. At the end of camp, we usually come back to our church for the final service and invite parents to attend. This allows the small group leaders and parents to connect once again and talk through the highlights of the weekend!

Small group leader-to-parent communication accomplishes a few powerful things:

1. Parents have greater buy-in with their child's small group because they know the leader personally and develop trust in their ability to lead their students well. As a result, the student's small group experience will be more consistent and even more power-

ful because their parents will support and prioritize their involvement in their group.

2. Parents gain extra support from the leader in the things they are trying to teach their child. Whether the student is a 4th grader in Kids Ministry or a 10th grader in Youth, when their small group leader knows what Mom and Dad are saying and working on at home, the leader can leverage their moments with students to reinforce the same things. In doing so, small group leaders can affirm to students that the wisdom their parents offer is valuable and important. This facilitates a sense of partnership and trust within the parent community and helps strengthen families.

3. Parents have greater access to personal pastoral care. I will never forget this playing out in a powerful way about a year ago. I had some family in town, and we were sitting on the floor of our living room playing a game. I began receiving phone calls and text messages from a couple different parents about a runaway student. I didn't know enough details to be able to step in myself at first, but I knew the young girl's small group leader, and I was able to make a quick phone call to her. I found out through that conversation that I was actually the last one to know about the missing student! The small group leader was already working together with the mom of the runaway student–and other parents from their small group–to support her in her efforts to find her daughter. The parents who had reached out to me

personally were just wanting to keep me in the loop. It was amazing to see how much support that mom had within our parent community with the help of her daughter's small group leader. ParentEquip Community at its finest.

This small group leader-to-parent line of communication really allows your ministry to scale with growth, providing the same level of care for families regardless of how big your ministry gets. This is essential for the body of Christ to operate as God intended: connection, community, and parent empowerment. Let me reiterate the importance of your small group leaders sharing their contact information with parents, just as I've encouraged you to share your own. Train your leaders well in this: Help them set boundaries. Remind them that it's healthy for them to not answer every call right away. But teach them that making themselves available to parents sets them up for greater impact on students–and on family units as a whole.

These lines of communication set your ministry up to practically carry out the vision of "family ministry," rather than just "kids" or "youth" ministry. When we recognize that our efforts in next gen ministry can help accomplish God's vision of parents operating as their kids' primary spiritual leaders, things will begin to change in a powerful way–and not just practically, but, I deeply believe, spiritually. When we step back into God's original strategy and design for discipleship, we will see His power at work in the lives of our students in a whole new way. In conclusion, it's not enough for us to simply communicate with parents. We must take a multifaceted approach, opening up these four lines of communication. When you do, you will begin to see the remarkable effects of the ParentEquip strategy in your ministry and within the families who are a part of it. We will be most effective when our communication is facilitated by an emphasis on community.

Chapter 6:
(Foundation #2)

Family Ministry
----(over)----
Kids / Youth Ministry

The second foundation of ParentEquip is all about our ministry mindset. I recently watched a photographer edit a group of photos, and in her editing process, I saw her apply a preset to all the photos. This preset created consistency with all the photos from her shoot, but still allowed each photo to remain unique. This mindset foundation is similar. Your ministry is made up of many different parts that allow you to impact kids or students, like incredible small groups, powerful worship (maybe even led by students!), fun events, camps, and perhaps missions trips. Your church might even do something like Fine Arts, where you steward and fan into flame the musical and artistic gifts of the young people in your ministry. All of these efforts are wonderful, and God uses them to transform the lives of the youth He's entrusted to you. But I want to suggest that these aspects of your ministry can be even more powerful if you consider how they can impact the whole family unit.

The mindset shift to FAMILY ministry instead of KIDS/YOUTH ministry starts with applying this question in all of the areas that make up your ministry: "How can we use _____ to bridge the gap between a child and their parents?" What I am suggesting in this chapter is not changing up your whole ministry model but, instead, adjusting your *filter* and vision for all the amazing things that you do. Your vision and motivation determine your actions and end result. What you decide to be your "why" will inform everything you do, so identifying the *right* "why" in your ministry is mission critical.

If I were to sit down with you in person and ask you what your ministry "why" is, you would likely say something along the lines of: "to see young people saved and following Jesus with their life." YES! Such a good "why." Maybe you would say something like, "to help young people know who they are in Christ and walk out their calling for the rest of their life." YES! Another great "why." While these are wonderful missions that are very much worth dedicating your life to, I would suggest that there is another layer to it–an even deeper "why."

So often, we approach ministry with the individual student in mind: leveraging our ministry to see students enter into personal relationships with Jesus, break through an addiction, redefine their identity and see themselves differently through the lens of Christ. While all of these things are great, the vision usually ends with the student. And while many of our kids and youth will grow up to impact the world for the sake of the Gospel, if we do not expand our vision beyond the individual student to their family as a whole, we will miss out on the opportunity to make an even greater impact.

I believe we could miss out on exponential impact for our ministries if we do not move back towards embracing God's design for the biblical family unit. If we align our ministry values with God's family design and see our ministry not just as a kids or youth ministry but a family ministry, we will reap a greater reward. As I said earlier in this book, I believe it's possible that the increasing number of unsaved parents in our world today is due to a failure in the Church to equip and empower **their** parents to embody their roles as spiritual leaders. The impact of church ministry has generational implications. What if the efforts you make today can actually change the future families of our world? I believe this can become possible if we focus not only on individual students but on the family of the student as well.

I want to share with you some practical ways to apply this filter of family impact in your ministry. You may already do some of these things, but applying this filter throughout your whole ministry will make way for a whole new level of impact.

Missions Trips - Let's say a particular "Youth" missions trip to Mexico has room for 32 people. In most churches, the trip would have a leader and a co-leader, and the rest of the group would be made up of students. Instead of taking two leaders and thirty young people, take your two leaders, twenty students, and **ten parents**. Allow students to see their parents serving people in a missions scenario. Create opportunities for them to work together for the Gospel. This changes the whole dynamic of the trip, and the resulting personal transformations can impact every corner of a family. Parents learn to lead spiritually; students learn to respect their parents' spiritual perspective. They're a team, linking arms in their walks with Christ. This is an incredible way to equip and partner with parents as they endeavor to step into their roles as spiritual leaders.

Small Groups - In certain ministry seasons at our church, we do something we call "BIGS." Each week that we have groups, we provide our leaders with a one-page document that consists of four "BIG" categories: (1) BIG Idea, (2) BIG Scripture, (3) BIG Story, and (4) BIG Questions. We've found that this small strategic document sets our leaders up to really dig in with their small groups in a powerful way. Providing a focused **idea statement** from that week's teaching, a **Scripture** that embodies the teaching, prompts for the leaders to share part of their **story** with the students, as well as 3-5 **questions** to start and steward the discussion time helps the leaders feel confident in their role. Because of the success we saw in this effort with small group leaders, we thought, "What would it look like for us to do the same for parents?" We began making a "sister-sheet" to the BIGS called "BIGS At Home." We shared the BIG Idea and BIG Scripture with parents, but encouraged parents to share their own BIG story with their kids and crafted additional BIG Questions, written with the parent in mind. Below is an example of the BIGS from one of our recent LifeGroups nights. On the left side, you can see the Leader BIGS for small groups. On the right side, you will see how we translated it to BIGS At Home.

Family Ministry Over Kids or Youth Ministry

THE 4 BIGS
April 15th, 2020

1. BIG IDEA	When I FOLLOW God, I don't have to walk in darkness
2. READ/ REFLECT *ask a student!*	John 8:12 [MSG] "Jesus once again addressed them: "I am the world's Light. <u>No one who follows me stumbles</u> around in the darkness. **I provide plenty of light to live in."** **How do we explain what darkness means in this?** Imagine the dungeon this earth would be without the light of the sun. <u>Just like the sun gives light to the earth, the SON of God (Jesus) gives light to the lives of His people.</u> This means that he frees our soul from darkness and helps us be free from the darkness sin brings throughout our life. <u>**This requires us to FOLLOW Christ.**</u>
3. Big Story *(for leaders)*	(Some of the leaders) Share one of three different things: 1. How your life felt **dark** BEFORE Christ 2. How following Christ **saved you from the consequences** that sin would have brought to you. 3. How you felt "darkness" **after making a mistake** and going against God. **(VULNERABLE)**
4. BIG QUESTION *(Spend 10-15 min)*	If students would like to answer one of the questions listed below, have them raise their hand in their video screen **and you can call on them when you choose!** • Have you ever seen someone make a decision that left them in a dark place? Have you ever been in that situation yourself? • How was your life BEFORE Christ? Can you tell that life feels brighter and more positive having a Savior? • How can you take a step **daily** to follow Christ and stay far from darkness? • Does anyone have any prayer requests? Lets pray! (Type your request in the chat here in ZOOM)

HAVE FUN IN YOUR ZOOM CHAT!

BIGS AT HOME
April 15th, 2020

1. BIG IDEA	When I FOLLOW God, I don't have to walk in darkness
2. READ/ REFLECT *ask a student!*	John 8:12 [MSG] "Jesus once again addressed them: "I am the world's Light. *No one who follows me stumbles* around in the darkness. *I provide plenty of light to live in.*" **How do we explain what darkness means in this?** Imagine the dungeon this earth would be without the light of the sun. *Just like the sun gives light to the earth, the SON of God (Jesus) gives light to the lives of His people.* This means that he frees our soul from darkness and helps us be free from the darkness sin brings throughout our life. ***This requires us to FOLLOW Christ.***
3. Big Story *(for parents)*	Parents - Share one of these three different things: (or more) 1. How your life felt **dark** BEFORE Christ 2. How following Christ **saved you from the consequences** that sin would have led you to. 3. How you felt "darkness" **after making a mistake** and going against God. **(VULNERABLE)**
4. BIG QUESTION *(Spend 10 min)*	Parents, remember that vulnerability from you can invite vulnerability from your teenager! • Have you ever seen someone make a decision that left them in a dark place? Have you ever been in that situation yourself? • How was your life BEFORE Christ? Can you tell that life feels brighter and more positive having a Savior? **(Maybe share your personal story of finding Christ)** • How can we as a family take a step **daily** to follow Christ and stay far from darkness? • What should we pray for right now? Any friends of yours need prayer? Can I pray for you?

SMALL STEPS MAKE A BIG DIFFERENCE!

Camps and Retreats—As I mentioned earlier, we always open our final camp service to parents, and I believe this really helps parents engage in the spiritual journey of their child. For our most recent camp, we ended our off-site camp experience with on onsite service at our main campus. We communicated dozens of times with parents beforehand, in the weeks leading up to camp, asking them to prioritize attending this service personally. I even used the word "mandatory" to express how important it was for parents to be there.

> **Side note:** *I believe that for this kind of language (that feels a bit extreme) to be well-received, you need to have strong relational equity with your parent community. They must know and trust your passionate and caring heart for their family. This only comes when you intentionally cultivate community with your parents.*

For this special final camp service, we have a special seating section for parents in the back of our auditorium. During the service, they get to see their kids passionately worship Jesus after a full weekend/week of camp. This often stirs up excitement in parents, because their children may have previously been passive about God and have now become passionate. Camps, man...they can do something special in a young person! We always ask our camp speaker to emphasize the importance of the post-camp journey in this last message. This helps us connect what God did in the life of a student during camp to the ongoing support role of a parent post-camp. We also always honor the parents in front of the students and acknowledge their role of spiritual authority in the students' lives. I will stand on stage before we dive into worship, ask the students to turn around and look at all the parents in the back, and ask them to honor and celebrate their parents.

Young people are growing up in a world today that is constantly taking shots at parents. We have lost the value of honor as a society. A great way to help bridge the gap between a parent and their child is to remind a young person how blessed they are to have a parent in their life who loves them and is doing the best they can to support them as they grow up.

Serve Projects—Similar to missions trips, serve projects are an incredible opportunity to mobilize students to serve and encourage parents to join, teaching them the power of serving as a family! This truly can have an impact that ripples out for generations to come. We are teaching young people who will one day become parents, and we have the chance to show them what it means to lead spiritually in the home. Creating opportunities for children to serve alongside their parents will bear lasting fruit.

Let's say your Kids Ministry is doing a Serve Night in preparation for Thanksgiving week. You will be assembling baskets filled with Thanksgiving meal supplies for families in need. Maybe the kids in your ministry will write letters and color pictures for the families. Why not include parents in this effort? Even a parent who does not believe in Jesus would probably join in on this! You never know what kind of seed might be planted in a parents' heart as they work to bless another family.

Discipleship and Scripture Memorization—I believe it's important for our Next Gen ministries to help facilitate discipleship beyond services and small groups. You can do this by designing study materials for students and their families to use during the week, like a Bible reading plan and a calendar for Scripture memorization. I encourage you to send parents weekly emails with devotions they can use to start discussions around the dinner table, along with a Scripture of the Week. Encourage parents to engage with the discipleship materials for their own spiritual development and to set a goal for the whole family to memorize the weekly Scripture. If we create these materials with the entire family in mind, we can help families grow spiritually, together.

In my monthly parent letters, I always include a section entitled "Call to Action" (see example below). In the Call to Action, I remind parents of their primary spiritual leader role, then give them straightforward, practical ideas to help them live out that calling over the next month. I send out new ideas each month, because the more I can activate parents to connect with their children as their spiritual leaders, the more I reinforce God's design for the family!

We recently started giving students trackers to help them keep tabs on their attendance and Scripture memorization. These trackers have space for the students to take notes on the weekly message as well. Our goal with these trackers is to get students to engage with messages on a deeper level, memorize 40 passages of Scripture, and attend 40 Wednesday night services throughout the year. We give parents these trackers as well, so that they can follow along with their students' Scripture memory schedule and engage them in discussion. Small, practical things like this can go a long way in equipping parents to be the leaders God has called them to be.

ParentEquip

Parent Letter
March 2021

A MESSAGE FROM PASTOR SAM:

"Hey Parents, I cannot believe we are already almost half way through February... can you believe it?! We are so excited about what is on the horizon for us. This next month is one we believe will mark your teenager FOREVER! We begin a series March 1st called "Will This Come Back to Haunt Me." It's all about Purity and Identity! Attached in this month's Parent Letter is a specific letter to you about this new series and an event we are doing following the series! Please continue to the final page to read it! **I deeply missed our monthly Parent Zoom Gathering in January so I'm excited to meet up again this month! Details below!**

STUDENT HIGHLIGHT: (Highlight a student here by giving their name, a picture of them and why they've stood out over the last month in your ministry. Get parent approval for using a photo)

Everyone meet _____!
  (Short highlight of student here)

WHAT'S UP THIS MONTH?

March 1st | **New Purity & identity Series** (Scroll to next page for more details)
March 19th | **Parent Zoom Gathering** 8:15pm (Info: Parent Community FB Page)
March 26th | **Purity Commitment Night** 5:30pm-7:00pm (At Broadcast Campus)
   ***Parents are highly encouraged to be a part of this service! Please mark it on your calendars! Check the Parent Facebook page for more info, and how to RSVP

WHAT'S UP THIS SEASON?

April 5th | **Summer Camp Registration Opens**
May 5th | **Cinco de Mayo MVMNT Night** (All Campuses at Kenosha)

If you'd like more information about any of these events, please don't hesitate to reach out to me personally at _____ or call my cell phone at _____.

CALL TO ACTION:
Your teenager needs YOU to help them walk out their faith, _more than you know_.
This month I'd love to encourage you to access God's call on your life to lead your teenager spiritually by doing these few things!

   1. **Keep reading our Group Bible Plans:** Regularly, we are diving into God's word as a ministry through shared Bible plans through the Bible App. This is a HUGE way for you to begin to take deeper steps into engaging with your teenager spiritually!
Go to our youth ministry website and click on "Click for Monthly Bible Plan" for direct link!
   2. **Join our March Parent Zoom Gathering:** On Sunday, March 19th we will be gathering together online for our monthly parent gathering. This is a GREAT place to meet other parents, get ministry updates as well as receive some encouragement. I would love for you to make this a priority! 8:15pm is when we will begin! Head to our Facebook page for Zoom link/details!
   3. **DO SOMETHING FUN - Shared Experiences are Powerful:** This month, try and prioritize a shared experience with each of your kids. It doesn't have to be expensive, but if you want it to be, go for it! Cost shouldn't be the focus - do something they would LOVE. This is a great opportunity to get into their world a little - showing interest in the things they enjoy is an easy way to deepen your connection with them!

MENTAL HEALTH RESOURCE:
We believe it is incredibly important to be mindful of mental health red flags in our lives as parents, and in the lives of our kids! If your family is in need of an excellent Christian counselor, please contact, (insert counselor's name and contact information here.)

Add photo of therapist here

Baptism—I know we all love creating environments for students to be baptized at camps, retreats, and special midweek services. But let me urge you to use the filter for family impact for every baptism opportunity. Baptism should be a family event, where parents and other family members gather to witness and support students as they take this important step in their faith journey. Have you ever attended a wedding ceremony where the officiant speaks to the wedding guests, exhorting them to commit to supporting the married couple throughout their lives? You have the same opportunity to engage the family in the spiritual development of their children during a baptism experience. Begin the baptism service with a brief explanation of the meaning of baptism, as well as a powerful encouragement of parents in their position as spiritual leaders from this moment forward. This will reinforce their understanding of God's design for spiritual discipleship within their family and give them a filter through which they see their children's journeys with Christ. Help them see that this is the moment to step into that leadership role more than ever before.

I really believe that the essential piece most next gen ministries are missing is engaging parents in everything they do. We shouldn't just consider parents in one area. We can't stop at weekly emails or monthly parent letters. There needs to be a shift in how we view all we do in our ministries. If we have parents on our minds, we will begin to leverage the influence of our ministry to support parents and reinforce their roles as primary spiritual leaders. We can be a part of seeing families come back in alignment with God's original design!

Applying the "Family Ministry Filter" will position your ministry to make a real difference in the long run. This difference won't be limited to your young people, or even their current family unit, but their future families as well, as they develop a biblical perspective on how they will one day parent their own children. Let me encourage you to zoom out. Your ministry isn't just affecting your students' lives today, or even a couple decades from now. We have to think and dream bigger! As leaders in the church today, we have the opportunity to change future generations of family units. There is no way to know the ripple of generational impact you can make by investing in the families of your ministry today.

Chapter 7: (Foundation #3)

Making Heroes
----(over)----
Being the Hero

Earlier in this book, I mentioned the concept of helping parents become "heroes of the faith" in their children's lives. That is the core idea behind this third foundation, and I would say that this is actually the core motivation behind the entire Parent-Equip strategy–to see parents setting the example, becoming a source of inspiration, becoming heroes to their children. And not just heroes but *spiritual* heroes, the people our students most look to for wisdom and guidance in their lives. We know from John 10:10 that the enemy is on mission to steal, kill and destroy, and certainly he focuses a lot of that effort on the next generation. I'm sure you see evidence of this regularly in your ministry. Throughout my time as a next generation pastor, I've come to firmly believe that his most effective destructive tactic is to target the family unit. We see the results of his efforts in so many more ways today than ever before.

Divorce rates are out of control. The LGBTQIA+ movement has skyrocketed gender dysphoria, which works directly against God's male and female design. More same-sex couples are parenting kids today than history has ever seen. In the last 50 years, the amount of single mothers raising kids has doubled. So many men are disengaged relationally from their kids or are completely absent from the home.

Another detrimental reality we see taking place in family units is parents staying married but having no intimacy or connection. These couples often only stay together until the kids graduate high school, then file for divorce. While these couples "stay together for the kids," it's almost guaranteed that the kids grew up seeing their parents grow apart. We've seen over the last decade that many adults are now choosing not to get married because of the unhappiness they witnessed in their parents' marriage growing up. When I coach married couples or teach at parent events, I always include one very specific piece of advice: to put every possible effort into making their marriage fun, rich, and intimate; to ensure they not only love each other, but also LIKE each other. I encourage them to prioritize date nights and show physical and emotional affection in front of their kids. I urge them to verbally encourage and affirm each other. Parents need to invest so intentionally in their marriage that there is no doubt in their kids' minds that Mom and Dad will be together forever. If we want to see this next generation experience remarkable marriages, we need to equip parents to *show them* remarkable marriages.

I believe that if the enemy can wreak havoc in the home, he increases his potential to do the same with the future families that come out of that home. Just as *God* thinks generationally, so does satan. In this foundation, I want to bring your attention to the three key components of ParentEquip Hero-Making:

1. We have to believe that parents *can* and *should* be the heroes in our students' lives.
2. We have to help parents believe they are heroes and equip them for heroism.
3. We have to help young people see their parents as heroes.

Each of these three components is imperative for the ParentEquip strategy. If one of these three are hindered or forgotten, the hero-making process becomes far less effective. I cannot overstate the importance of this aspect of ParentEquip. Our efforts in this area have the potential to affect families for a lifetime–and generations to come.

Believing the parent should be the HERO

As next generation leaders, we are cool. We know it. We've got the language, we've got the shoes, we most likely still enjoy the same things our students enjoy, right? Ok...maybe we're not always actually "cool"...but you get the point. We work to stay relevant to our students. One of the greatest opportunities we have with young people is that in their teen years, they typically try to pull away from their parents and venture out to hear different voices. In this phase of their life, they begin stepping into their independence more and more; they begin forming their own, more concrete beliefs about all kinds of things. And because they are beginning to become their "own person," in a way, they may start to believe that their parents "don't understand them" anymore, the way other people might. This belief often causes students to seek us out as "outside voices" and gives us the opportunity to begin speaking into their lives. As next generation leaders, this is a wonderful thing! And it's vital that we leverage this newfound influence to redirect students to their parents and reinforce the family unit.

Do you remember growing up and hearing Mom or Dad tell you the same advice over and over again...but you still didn't listen? Then, another adult you admired gave you the same advice and you thought it was revolutionary! This is incredibly common because of the natural "detachment" that happens between a parent and a teen during this phase of a teen's life. While this is normal, the enemy will try to use this stage as an opportunity to disconnect a child from their parents for good. As parents get frustrated that their child doesn't listen to them and sees them listening to other adults, it can cause a huge rift between the parents and the student. The parents' reaction to this shift in their relationship, if not handled properly, can push a teen further away. This perpetuates a cycle of their children seeking out other people for guidance and wisdom that chronically deepens the divide.

There are two parents in our ministry who really inspire me when it comes to this subject in particular: Jon and Janet Brown. You actually may have heard of Jon, because he has been in youth ministry for over two decades and is sought out by next generation leaders all over the country for insight, wisdom and mentoring. But beyond their impact in next generation ministry, Jon and Janet are remarkable parents. They blow me away. I actually initially met Jon because I reached out to him in 2019 in a particular season when I felt like I was falling short as a father. He was a seasoned next generation pastor, and I had admired him from afar, so I wanted to gain some wisdom from him. Just months later, I joined his staff and began leading his youth ministry.

Jon and Janet are the type of parents all of us wish we had. They are fun, full of the Holy Spirit, excited about life and focused on giving their three daughters the best life possible. They travel multiple times a year as a family, do daddy/mother-daughter dates on the regular. On their way to school each morning, they pray with their girls for a large list of missionaries their family supports. They have the tough conversations with other parents when a boy enters the picture. And for something as simple as a sleepover, they are "over"-protective and take care to guard their girls to the best of their ability.

Those are all great things, but they do something else that I know Elizabeth and I will for sure do with our children: They walk each of their girls through a season of praying for a group of female mentors who they want to invest in them. During this process, they encourage the girls to pray for ladies they admire and want to be like. Jon and Janet pray with the girls as well. After some time, the girls make a list (every time, it's a list of remarkable women who meet Jon and Janet's approval), and they pursue those relationships. This has been a game changer for their family, because as they have grown, their girls have already begun to pull back from Jon and Janet, even though they are *phenomenal* parents. It's just an inevitable progression for every student. Guaranteed.

Often, the things that are inevitable intimidate us as parents and, frankly, paralyze us. Knowing that one day our kids will pull away from us in their pursuit of independence is daunting. But here's a really important truth: When something is inevitable, we can plan for it and leverage it in a way that is beneficial for our children. Jon and Janet have done this, and the girls they are raising are absolutely incredible, not only because of Jon and Janet, but because of the half dozen or so mentors in each of their lives.

As next generation leaders, we have to be aware of the inevitable tension points that parents walk through and use our influence and perspective to help them prepare in advance. By working through these challenging seasons with parents, rather than solely with students, we can help equip parents to continue to be the primary spiritual leaders in their families, even when their children go through phases when they naturally pull away. I think all of us as ministry leaders have something in us that makes us want to be heroes in the lives of our students, in a way, but I believe true heroism is positioning parents to be seen as their children's heroes! I often try to point my students back to their parents with statements like "I just finished talking to your mom about you. She is so proud of who you are. It's so evident she loves you," or, "I observed your dad watching you preach Sunday morning in middle school. It couldn't be more obvious that he is captivated by you and so very proud of how you're stepping into your calling."

Just recently, we had a girl in our youth ministry express her deep desire to go to our Winter Camp, and I asked her why she was unable to join. She said she was behind in school and her dad didn't understand why she could be so passionate about church but not give an adequate effort in her academics. I asked her if she had been trying hard over the past couple months, and she was quick to admit that she really hadn't applied herself at school. I told her this: "While you want to go to camp, it's obvious that it's a high priority for your dad to see you succeed in school. That is because he loves you and wants you to have the best possible future. I want to encourage you to go home tonight and talk to your dad. Let him express his concerns, and listen respectfully. Make a commitment to him that you're going to follow through and work hard in school, and see what he says." That night, she texted me and said that she had just finished talking with her dad. She had apologized for being behind in school and expressed that she understood and appreciated her father's concern. She'd asked if it would be possible for her to go to camp if she caught up on all of her work and committed to raise each of her grades a full grade level before the end of the semester, and he'd agreed. As a result, she went to camp, followed through on that commitment to her dad, and now she wants to join our ministry college.

As next generation leaders, the ultimate win is not for us to live heroically for the people the Lord has entrusted to us. I do think in some ways they may see us as heroes, and that is, of course, ok! But let me propose that the ultimate win is leveraging our influence to build relationships between students and their parents and let the parents become the real heroes.

The Obvious Tension: Not all parents are "heroic"

There is a family in our church that truly inspires me. The Helzer family is made up of a set of super engaged parents, three very athletic sons and a precious young daughter who may end up being president one day. If I could write a book that adequately expressed how these parents steward each of their four kids, it would be a number-one best seller in days. I'm always captivated by watching the Helzers parent. They are encouragers, constantly drawing out their children's best gifts. They are intentional with spending one-on-one time with each of their kids and giving them focused attention. They prioritize church, no matter the busyness of their season. They put a great deal of time and effort into their marriage. I could go on and on. When I watch them, I cannot help but believe that their kids see them as heroes, and if one of them doesn't for some reason, one day they will. I believe parents like the Helzers are a great picture of what the Lord desires parents to be in the life of their children. When I think about the ministry I lead, as well as yours, I long for us to help this world have more parents like the Helzers.

But even as I type this, I am conflicted. When I look at our world today, I struggle with believing that it's even possible to make this the "norm." After more than ten years of youth ministry, I have seen such a large number of disengaged, distant, or completely absent parents...and it still sometimes makes me question if we can turn that around. I know that because we live in a fallen world, there will always be some parents who remain disengaged. But I want to establish a belief that is crucial to the success of ParentEquip. Honestly, if we don't get this right, we will not be able to build our ministries on this foundation. While not every parent in our ministry can be a Jon or Janet, or a Helzer, we have to believe this truth: Every parent has heroism inside of them.

A single mom who is working three jobs to survive and is completely disengaged relationally from her child has heroism within her. Her son or daughter might resent Mom for being absent, but we can help them navigate those feelings by highlighting the heroic effort she is making to provide for them. That dad who is overprotective and, at times, a bit angry–he doesn't always look like a hero. But we can use our influence with his daughter to remind her of his passion to keep her safe: that while he may be a bit overbearing, he may just be afraid to see something bad happen to her. He may not be expressing his love and care in a way that draws his daughter close, but he loves her nonetheless. If we can help highlight the father's love for his daughter, and maybe even find some intentional time with Dad to help him process some of what he is feeling and how he is displaying those feelings, we can help build a powerful relational bridge between them.

I've rarely found a parent who didn't have some sort of heroism in them. It may take work to mine that gold in them, and to change your own mindset about them, but my prayer is that you would adopt this perspective. **You will never be a true hero-maker if you don't see parents as heroes.** Champion parents in the eyes of their children by highlighting their strengths. For those parents who don't embody heroism yet, draw out their great qualities. Build equity with them so you can begin to minister to them as parents. You'll begin to see some incredible things shift. Wouldn't you agree that many parents (if not the majority) feel like they just can't get it right when it comes to their kids? Well, encourage them and then equip them to be who God has called them to be. Let's be advocates to parents as well as for them to their kids.

All that is to say, I know not every parent has it all together and embodies the heroism we hope to see in parents. But that does not excuse us from our responsibility to passionately pursue parents in effort to fan into flame their God-wiring to be a hero. I've seen this effort impact families in remarkable ways for years, and I believe you will see it, too. I want to close out this chapter by identifying some of the reasons why parents might not currently function as spiritual heroes in their children's lives. My hope is that these perspectives will influence you to reimagine the way you view the parents that make up your ministry.

1. **Some parents don't know they are called by God to be the primary spiritual leaders for their kids.** Most parents are not intentionally neglecting this role. As I mentioned earlier in this book, I believe the way the local church has functioned over the last many decades has created a reality in which many parents don't know their role in God's design for families. While at times we get frustrated with parents for not leading in their home, we tend to forget to assess how our internal systems and church history have contributed to parents missing their mark. So, instead of carrying frustration or just writing off parents for their regular "misses," we should accept the

responsibility for helping change the way parents see their role. We should step up with passion to help educate parents and cast vision as to why this is such a significant mantle for them to pick back up! Teaching a parent about their inner heroism is one of the most important and heroic things we could ever do as next generation leaders.

2. **Some parents don't follow Jesus themselves.** While this may seem like an obvious one, this is one of the biggest excuses we use as next generation leaders to avoid engaging with parents. Lost parents tend to be a "free pass" for us to focus solely on the student without effort to impact the entire family. Here is what I believe is one of the most important perspectives you'll read in this entire book: *Your care and passion for a student is one of your greatest evangelistic tools to shepherd a mom or dad to Jesus.* The majority of parents feel drawn to people who love and care for their children.

Let me share an experience I had a few years ago that really drove this home for me. I had two students in my ministry named Alexis and Jermaine. Both were unsaved, and it was obvious they came from a home that had not yet been infiltrated by the Gospel of Jesus. Alexis and Jermaine began attending our youth ministry during our annual evangelistic series that attracted hundreds of students to our ministry. Their mom, Sophia, was the type of mom that dropped her kids off super early at church (making Alexis and Jermaine honorary set-up crew members) and, at times, forgot to pick them up at the end of the night. I remember taking Jermaine home one evening to find out that his mom just didn't want to get out of bed to come get him.

Sophia was very much disengaged, but I believed there were some heroic attributes within her. I got Sophia's cell phone number and began to contact her directly about different events and activities I wanted Alexis and Jermaine to join in on. While her kids could have found out about upcoming events in a number of other ways, I knew that a personal connection with Mom would make a long term impact. As we discussed in the first foundation, there is power in a parent having your cell number. After a while, Sophia began showing up to the church and, instead of dropping her kids off, she would get out of the car and walk them inside. Same thing for pick up at the end of the night. She began to come around more, and I knew that God was doing something within her.

After several months of building relationships with this family, I could see Alexis' and Jermaine's interest in attending one of our annual camps growing, and I was excited to see what God could do in their life over a powerful camp weekend. When camp came around, I worked with Sophia personally. While we had a large amount of students attending our camp, I knew that my individualized connection to Sophia and her kids would make an impact in the long run.

What happened at camp was very unexpected–and it's probably not what you're thinking. First, I have to say Jermaine *flourished*. I watched him dive deep into relationships. Small groups were SUPER impactful for him, and he grew in ways I hadn't seen in prior months. I believe the

Lord was stirring some incredible things within him. Alexis, on the other hand, had a very different experience. Over my years in youth ministry, I've only had to send two students home from a camp. Yes, only two. Alexis, unfortunately, was my number two.

Alexis really struggled to assimilate into a small group that weekend. She had some anxiety that totally monopolized her small group leader's time, creating tensions within the group. She also chose not to take her medication for consecutive days, leading her to act out in some inappropriate ways. Sadly, I had to call Sophia and let her know what was happening, which involved me asking her to drive two hours to pick up Alexis and take her home early. I'll never forget seeing Jermaine's disappointment, as well as hearing Sophia's tone shift on the phone. I could tell she wasn't angry, but her heart was broken.

This is the point in the story that really drives home the impact of this ParentEquip foundation: When Sophia arrived at camp, I remember watching her get out of her car and walk up to Alexis. She didn't respond with anger or condemnation, but with compassion. I guarantee she never would have responded that way in the past. She went from being completely disengaged and very stand-offish, just months prior, to attentive, present, and gracious. As I watched that encounter take place between Sophia and her daughter, it was clear to me that the Lord had been doing a work in her.

Some might not think this change was particularly substantial, but I really believe it was. Sophia walked up to me, apologized and thanked me for caring for her kids. When Alexis and Jermaine had first started attending our church, she wouldn't even look at me through the car window when I stood outside every week to try and catch her attention to begin a conversation. But on this day, I could see in her eyes a deep appreciation for what our ministry was doing for her kids, and, really, for her family. I share this story with you because I want to illustrate that even your lost parents are part of your mission. It's not your lead pastor's job to save adults on the weekend while you focus on the teens. It's a combined effort by all the leaders in your church to see families changed forever. So if you have parents in your ministry who seem totally hands-off and even unreachable, I want to urge you to lean into the opportunity you have to create change in their families for today, and for the eternal.

3. **Some parents want to lead spiritually, but they don't know how.** Let me share with you a significant truth that is often missed: Parents who desire to lead spiritually don't ask for help as much as they should. If we wait to hear from well-intentioned parents who do want to lead their kids spiritually, we will likely be waiting forever. It's honestly rare to find a group of parents who are vocal about their desire to lead. They're either embarrassed to ask for help or don't really understand the resource we can be for them. This is why it's so important for us to be proactive in our equipping strategies!

Say you're on a fishing trip, and the tide is perfect, the current is flowing the exact way it should, and, due to the time of day, the fish are ready to bite. In your boat, you've got the fishing poles ready and lines baited, but instead of casting them in the water, you slide them into the holders on the side of the boat, leaving the hooks dangling feet above the water with bait that would guarantee a catch. You might sit back, sip on a drink and enjoy the sun, but no fish will be caught that day, regardless of the fishes' hunger, because you never tossed in the bait. We do this with hungry parents all the time! We might not know which ones they are or how long they've been around the church, but they're there. And if we don't make the effort to "cast" and provide what they are yearning for, we will be unsuccessful in helping them step into that primary spiritual leader role. Don't wait for parents to pursue you. Instead, choose a proactive approach, and mold your ministry philosophy around what is called *"cueing"* parents.

"Cueing" parents is a concept developed by a team at Orange called ParentCue. ParentCue is one of the efforts I admire most in the entire ministry world. **Their team is the greatest parent-equipping team on the planet.** I have used their tools for years and will continue for the rest of my life. The philosophy of "cueing" parents is similar to the way a personal trainer "cues" an athlete. They give specific, proactive instruction to help their athletes lift safely and grow stronger with every workout. If we take a proactive approach to equipping parents, we can set them up for success as they take on the challenge and calling of being the primary spiritual leaders in their children's lives. Here are a few practical ways to begin proactively equipping parents in your ministry:

- ~ Create discussion questions for parents to use to engage their kids on the drive home from church. Parents often don't just lack the WHAT, they also lack the WHEN. Set them up to win by providing questions for them before service even begins so they can prepare a bit before the car ride home.

~ Organize a monthly parent letter like I mentioned previously, including monthly challenges for the parents. I've seen huge success with parent letters–they're a great part of the ParentEquip strategy. Utilize the template I've included in the appendix to help you draft your own. In that letter, you'll find a variety of details, from student highlights to schedules, as well as that monthly parent "Call to Action." I love to give parents creative ideas for how they can engage with their children as their spiritual leaders. One of my favorite ideas is writing encouragement for their child on a sticky note each day of that week or month and placing it somewhere their kid will see it often. This could be an encouraging word the parent feels they hear from God about their child, or a specific Scripture. Simple, but significantly impactful.

~ Purchase and hand out a book or resource that you believe will benefit many of the parents in your ministry. I encourage you to purchase that resource in bulk and either give it away or provide it at a super discounted price. I did this not too long ago with my brother-in-law Will Hutcherson's book, Seen, which he wrote with a wonderful licensed therapist, Dr. Chinwe Williams. Seen was written to help parents and church leaders as they work to support young people who are struggling with their mental health. If you haven't read *Seen* yet, you absolutely have to! Check it out at theseenbook.com

When *Seen* released, I ordered over a hundred copies and made them available for purchase for $5. (Of course, this was a financial sacrifice for our ministry, but it was absolutely worth it for what our families gained!) Within the first week, we had sold and given out dozens of copies of the book. This was a powerful way to be proactive in equipping parents in a relevant and timely topic. From conversations with a few parents who were willing to bring it up, I knew there were at least a handful of students in our ministry who were struggling mentally–and I'm sure there were many more. Other parents were in the same boat but weren't quite ready to speak up. Instead of waiting to see more parents reach out for help, I took a step that I knew would be a huge support for all of our families. I've heard from many parents that *Seen* has really helped them walk with their child through mental health struggles. So, whatever resource God lays on your heart, be sure to share it with the parents in your ministry! It could be a blog, a short YouTube video, or even a small quote you see on social media.

~ Do a group devotional on the Bible app. This tool is powerful, accessible to everyone, and largely untapped for the purposes of equipping parents and building relational equity with them. This can be a part of your multifaceted communication strategy that we talked about earlier in this book. If you create space for your leaders, your students and their parents to all do a public devotional together, the fruit will blow your mind. We did a few back-to-back devotionals like this a couple years ago, and my only regret was that we hadn't done it sooner! When students comment in the "talk it out" section of the devo, parents like their comments or comment for themselves, and leaders engage as well, it's just so powerful. Try it! It will bring parent-equipping in your ministry to a whole new level! Just think of the conversations this will prompt between students and parents throughout the week.

All of these practical steps can help the parents in your ministry become spiritual heroes in the eyes of their children. That's what it's all about! While it's a great thing for young people to see church leaders as heroes, it's so important for us to leverage our influence to build up a parent's heroic nature. Whether or not they embody it fully today, we can still draw it out of them and help their kids see who God has always wanted their parents to be in their life!

Part Three: The Application

Chapter 8:
The Fruit of ParentEquip in Your Ministry

While this whole book thus far has been focused on the impact the strategy will make outside your ministry (in the home), it's time to talk about how your ministry will benefit. The strategy of ParentEquip will bring about some truly incredible things in your ministry! God blesses what we do when we reinforce what He designed. In this chapter, I'll lay out some of the tangible, likely results you'll see as you implement the strategies we've discussed throughout the book. I hope this will even further convince you to take some bold steps with the ParentEquip strategy. I again want to encourage you that this is a "long haul" strategy. It will take time to see some of the results mentioned below. In some contexts, six to twelve months will be enough time to produce evident fruit. For others, it may take longer than that. Don't be discouraged. Stick with the vision and mission of ParentEquip. You will eventually see families impacted and ministry growth because of your efforts! While deeply connecting a child to their parent is the ultimate goal of this strategy, you will certainly see benefits across your ministry as well. Some of what I mention below will be familiar because we touched on it in previous chapters, but I believe in those cases, it's worth repeating.

Camp Sign-Ups & Engagement

When you get parents on board with at what your ministry is trying to accomplish, parents will prioritize their child's engagement in your ministry. Over time, you will see your camp sign-ups not only grow in number, but you'll see camp sign-ups come in more *quickly*. The more parents are engaged, the more responsive they are. The days of your students having to convince their parents to let them attend a camp may not be completely over, but you'll see fewer parents pushing back on the sign-up process. You will also see an increase of parent engagement in serving opportunities leading up to camp, during camp, and post-camp. For one of our most recent camps, we needed three different groups of parents to serve throughout the weekend. Getting the help we needed was easy, because so many parents were excited to play a part in such a formative weekend! And by the way, some of the parents who served were unbelievers who had an opportunity to serve alongside other incredible parents who had an evident relationship with Jesus–another incredible evangelistic opportunity for your ministry!

The Fruit of ParentEquip in Your Ministry

Fewer Angry Parents

I think all of us next generation leaders could use a bit of this "fruit" that flows from the ParentEquip strategy. As you build relationship with your Parent Community, you'll find more parents filled with "benefit of the doubt" rather than rage (ha!). When parents feel connected to you as a leader and connected to the ministry you lead, they will be significantly less likely to jump to conclusions. Over my last five years of ministry, I've seen a massive decrease of angry/frustrated parents, because I've implemented this ParentEquip strategy. Today, I rarely encounter an angry parent, and when I do, they don't stay angry for long!

More Consistent Attendance for Individual Students

In most youth ministries, students attend an average of 2 services per month. As you embrace the ParentEquip strategy, you'll see that number increase! While parents can be the greatest support for getting a student to church, they can also be the greatest hindrance. If you begin to activate parents through this strategy, you'll see a greater commitment from the parent, which will lead to a more consistent student. This will eventually produce a greater overall monthly attendance average for your ministry!

An Influx of New Families Joining your Church

This has been one of the most consistent outcomes of the ParentEquip strategy. In Part 1 of this book, we discussed the power of creating a Parent Community. Over the years,

I have seen hundreds of new families join the churches I served due to the intentional parent connections being made by the youth ministry. I just recently talked with a youth pastor who's been getting some pressure from his pastor to grow his youth ministry. The numbers aren't where his pastor wants them to be. I'm coaching this youth pastor through the ParentEquip strategy, and I expect to see not only his youth ministry increase numerically, but overall weekend attendance as well. It actually works! Building a Parent Community with the ParentEquip strategy could be a game changer for both your next generation ministry and for your church as a whole.

More Parents Serving in your Ministry

I recognize that not every next generation ministry has a culture of parents serving, but I believe parent volunteers are incredible assets. There are so many students growing up without Christlike examples as parents (which, of course, is a reality we hope to change), so if you can fill your ministry with godly parents who can take those students under their wings, you'll see some wonderful benefits. The ParentEquip strategy will cultivate a greater parent volunteer culture. They'll see the impact your ministry makes on their family, and they will want to be a part of impacting other families with you!

Chapter 9:
Leading Your Ministry Forward

Your next steps are pivotal. The world is shifting and showing no signs of stopping, and many parents are feeling like they are losing out to culture. Many others have given up altogether. The opportunity to reconcile the family back to its original design is right in front of us. I deeply believe the Lord is looking for leaders who are willing to be passionate about the family again. Continuing next generation ministry without engaging and equipping parents cannot remain the norm. While what you do may seem to be working, if you're not engaging parents, it's simply not as effective as it could be. I implore you to really weigh all that you've read in this book. My prayer is that you will at least take some steps forward and try this strategy out.

Below are a few key next steps to help you embrace ParentEquip and lead your ministry forward with an emphasis on God's design for families. Let's reinstate parents as the spiritual leaders God has always called them to be!

1. **Share ParentEquip with your lead pastor.** Your lead pastor is the person who carries the full vision for your church, and it's so important for you to have their support and backing as you pursue these new strat-

egies. Have them read the book or give a summary of the three foundations, and then discuss how the ParentEquip strategy could impact your church today. To implement Parent-Equip effectively, you need to move forward as a unified team!

2. **Get your staff and volunteer team on board.** Your ParentEquip efforts will only go as far as the leaders in your ministry will carry them. It's crucial for your team to be all in with the philosophy! If you'd like for me to do a coaching session with your team, please reach out to me. I would love to help your leaders catch the vision! I'm available for coaching both onsite or via Zoom. A session like this can help get your team unified around the vision, energized like never before, and ready to start running in this new direction! I urge you to also read through this book together as a team.

3. **Start building your Community.** Your Parent Community is deeply foundational for this strategy. The best way to begin building it right now is to create a Facebook group. Start gathering parents virtually, consolidate your communication in one place, and then begin to cultivate the multifaceted communication I talked about in Part 1. It will take time to implement the different tiers of communication, because it will require some culture shifting and team training. Let me encourage you to just start and embrace the process. Start training your volunteers to engage parents, and begin cultivating a culture of parents connecting with each other. And make

yourself accessible. Here we go...give out your cell phone number! Set those boundaries, but let parents be able to reach out to you in a personal way. Each of these pieces of your communication and Parent Community strategy will make a huge difference. Just take it one step at a time.

4. **Host a Parent Night at one of your youth services.** Set a date about a month or two out for parents to join in on a service. Do not expect an excessive amount of parents; it will probably take 3-5 of these services for you to start seeing some encouraging numbers. Don't give up. Remember: ParentEquip is a long-game approach. It will rarely (if ever) produce overnight success, but it will ultimately bear fruit that lasts.

5. **Set a goal to meet with a couple of parents every week.** The more you make yourself available to parents, the more parents will reach out to you. But begin with pursuit. Reach out first and grab some coffee, or invite them to come hang out with you in your church lobby. Ask them some thoughtful questions to show your care not only for their child, but for them as parents and their family as a whole. For example, you could ask:

    ◆ "Are there any specific things you're trying to teach your student that I could help reinforce when I am around them?"

    ◆ "I recognize that parenting in our world today is very tough. How can I be praying for you specifically to help support you as you walk alongside your student?"

- ◆ Never underestimate the power of face-to-face connection. Listen well, and make sure they know you want to see them succeed as a parent!

6. **Begin calling out and celebrating the heroism in the parents in your ministry.** It's often said in the church world, "Whatever is rewarded is repeated." Affirming heroism in parents will spur them on to continue to show up and lead their children. Write them letters. Tell their kids what you see in their parents. As they walk through the lobby at your church or when you see them at a grocery store, stop and uplift them with an encouraging word. This will edify them greatly! And you'll find that the more you do this over time, the more your heart will begin to shift towards parents. You'll begin to have an increased desire to see them succeed. God will bless that!

These are some good starting points, but it's just the beginning. You have months and years of greater impact ahead of you! Let me encourage you one more time to embrace the process. It takes time to implement the ParentEquip strategy, but it is so worth it. I would love to journey alongside you as you walk this out, whether it's through individual coaching, team coaching, having me join you for one of your parent events or simply connecting in our ParentEquip Community on our Facebook page. I would love to support you and be a resource for you.

While I believe in parents as their children's primary spiritual leaders, I believe deeply in the leaders who God is positioning to impact the family unit through next generation ministry. I pray that you would experience the massive blessing of God on your life and over your own family as you help bridge the gap between children and their parents, ultimately reconciling the family unit back to what God desired and intended it to be from the beginning!

Welcome to the ParentEquip Family!

Sources:

"You lost me" - Page 23 (59% stat)

"Faith for Exiles" - Page 15 (Increase from 59% to 64% stat)

https://www.census.gov/library/stories/2021/04/number-of-children-living-only-with-their-mothers-has-doubled-in-past-50-years.html

https://williamsinstitute.law.ucla.edu/publications/same-sex-parents-us/

https://nickcady.org/2016/06/20/the-impact-on-kids-of-dads-faith-and-church-attendance/